D1108785

MARIA S. BROUSCARIS

THE MONUMENTS OF THE ACROPOLIS

ARCHAEOLOGICAL GUIDE

GENERAL DIRECTION OF ANTIQUITIES AND RESTORATION
ATHENS, 1978

GUIDES : No 39

1, Tositsa Str., Athens 147
Editor : A. Kaloyeropoulou
Translated by A. Doumas
Original edition : A. Ninou
Art editor : Louisa Montesantou

Printed by «Atlantis - M. Pechlivanides & Co», S.A.

Illustration of the cover : Parthenon seen from the Propylaea

CONTENTS

PREFACE

To describe the monuments of the Acropolis, to analyse their aesthetic value as befits them and to narrate their historic vicissitudes from the moment of their birth until the present day would surely require whole volumes. These very subjects have been dealt with extensively in a host of specialised monographs and studies by innumerable scholars, historians, archaeologists, aestheticians, architects and others. The aim of the present guide is more limited. Fully aware of the heavy responsibility of those who «take on» the Acropolis, I have attempted to furnish the visitor who is certainly not restricted to a quick, superficial and usually indifferent glance, the visitor who comes to the Acropolis with questions and seeks their immediate answer without being obliged to resort to libraries, even the visitor who comes to pay homage to the monuments in his nostalgia for the past, some assistance for an initial acquaintance. This guide includes the historical context, general description of the monuments which have survived as well as those which have disappeared and have but left their traces upon the rock, some testimonies of ancient visitors concerning the monuments and the now-lost votives which once of a day filled the area and, finally, a brief aesthetic analysis of those principles which distinguish the Parthenon and the other monuments of the Acropolis as unrivalled works of art.

It is evident that, whoever wishes to learn more and to penetrate further must have recourse to the general text-books and specific studies which have been written about the Acropolis and its monuments in abundance. To give a detailed catalogue of them is outside both the scope and the limits of this guide. However, it is useful to mention some, very few, without implying that the omission of others means they are less worthy since, indeed, we note that among the studies not expressly mentioned there are some which have contributed considerably to our knowledge and understanding of the monumental heritage of the Acropolis. Regrettably we are unable to refer to them and confine ourselves to mentioning just a few of the most important books.

Before this bibliographical note, I think it necessary to say a few words about the ancient sources which speak of the rock and its monuments as these are the nearest testimonies. Perhaps the most valuable of all are the inscriptions referring to buildings or votives for these texts are public documents. Important information is contained in the surviving works of some ancient authors, for instance Herodotus, Thucydides, Xenophon, Demosthenes, Plutarch and others. With the mythical and historical traditions of Athens and the Acropolis dealt the so-called Attic-Chroniclers (Atthidographs) whose works, however, have been almost completely lost. Fortunately for us one such work has survived; by a traveller of the Imperial period, Pausanias of Lydia in Asia Minor, who described Central Greece and the Peloponnese in about the middle of the 2nd century A.D. His work has no literary merit whatsoever being a hotch-potch of descriptions of cities and monuments, of historical events and mythical tradition, but precisely because of the quantity of information it contains it is especially valuable. Pausanias saw Greece as it was almost at the close of its ancient life, before the barbarian invasions, the religious fanaticism and political expediency even of Byzantium, dealt their mortal blows. The information given us by medieval authors concerning the fate of the Acropolis during the long interval from the close of Antiquity until Modern times is comparatively negligible and invariably confused.

Modern times for the Acropolis may be said to commence with the arrival of travellers from the West. The information they give and, in particular, their sketches are of inestimable value especially the drawings which were made prior to the destruction of the monuments. We mention only Carrey, Fourmont, Stuart and Revett, Gell, Cole, Spon, Wheler, Dalton.

Whoever wishes to find the information left us by the ancient and medieval authors, the inscriptions speaking of the Acropolis which had been discovered by the turn of the century, Pausanias' description of the Acropolis and, finally, a brief survey of its adventures in recent times, must resort to the fundamental book of O. Jahn and A. Michaelis, Arx Athenarum, published in Bonn 1901.

Another monumental work of about the same period is Ἡ Ἀνασκαφὴ τῆς Ἀκροπόλεως, 1906, by P. Kavvadhias and G. Kawerau (German architect). This includes a systematic description of the Acropolis and a general picture of the excavation conducted over its whole area between 1885 and 1890, which revealed, among others, the artistic treasures of the Archaic period.

A synthetic picture of some of the Classical monuments on the Acropolis is given in Ch. Picard's edition, L' Acropole. Here are described the ramparts, the entrance to the Acropolis, the Nike Bastion and the Propylaea. The wonderful illustrations immortalise the appearance of the Acropolis and its environs at the turn of the century.

The oldest systematic work written about the Parthenon is Penrose' book, Principles of Athenian Architecture, printed by the Dilettanti Society of London in 1851.

A much more recent publication of the history, architecture and sculptural decoration of the Parthenon is included in M. Collignon's book, Le Parthénon, 1912.

A monumental publication on the architecture of the Parthenon is being completed by Professor and Academician A. Orlandos; and printed by the Archaeological Society. A first volume, the plates, has been issued (1977).

Concerning the sculptures of the Parthenon, especially worthy of mention is, first and foremost, A. H. Smith's monumental publication, British Museum, The Sculptures of the Parthenon, 1910. Fr. Brommer has systematically published in recent years the pediments, Die Skulpturen der Parthenongiebel, 1963, the metopes, Die Metopen des Parthenon, 1967. The frieze has just been issued (1977).

The great edition of G. Ph. Stevens, L. Caskey, H. Fowler and J. Paton, The Erechtheum, 1927, exhausts the history, architecture and sculpted decoration of this edifice. The diverse cult themes associated with this peculiar building are considered by N. Kontoleon in his book: Τὸ Ἐρέχθειον ὡς Οἰκοδόμημα Χθονίας Λατρείας, an edition of the Athens Archaeological Society no. 29, 1949.

A systematic description of the Propylaea was given a century ago by R. Bohn in his book, Die Propyläen der Akropolis zu Athen, 1882. More recently Bundgaard (a Swedish architect), examined different problems which the building poses and evaluated (not always flatteringly) the personality of Mnesicles in his book of that name published in 1957.

The remains of the poros buildings of the Archaic period were first discussed by Th. Wiegand in his book, Die Poros-Architektur der Akropolis zu Athen, 1904, while their sculptures were dealt with by R. Heberdey in his book, Altattische Porosarchitektur, 1919.

By studying the roof tiles found on the Acropolis, E. Buschor distinguished buildings and constructional phases of buildings of the Archaic, Classical and post-Classical period. His book, Die Tondächer der Akropolis, was printed by the German Institute of Athens in 1929.

In one of his books, H. Payne (Archaic Marble Sculpture from the Acropolis) gave a refreshing picture of these works of art. These were also the subject of the monumental publication of H. Schrader, E. Langlotz and W. H. Schuchhardt, Die archaischen Marmorbildwerke der Akropolis, 1939, which covered the whole wealth of works then existing in the form of a systematic catalogue.

The inscriptions from the Acropolis and from Athens in general are basically published in the first volumes of the enormous edition of the Prussian Academy of Letters, entitled Inscriptiones Graecae, as well as in its supplementary volumes. A systematic catalogue of the dedicative inscriptions of the 6th and 5th centuries B.C. is given by A. Raubitschek in his book, Dedications from the Athenian Acropolis, 1949.

We now know, far better than ever before, what the Acropolis was like in Mycenaean times thanks to the scrutinizing study of Sp. Iakovidhes whose conclusions were published in his book, Ἡ Μυκηναϊκὴ Ἀκρόπολις τῶν Ἀθηνῶν, 1962 (Doctoral Thesis).

One can read about the historical vicissitudes of the Acropolis and of the Parthenon in particular in Medieval and Recent times in J. Baelen's book, La Chronique du Parthénon, 1956.

N. Balanos, an architect, described and drew in his book Ἡ Ἀναστήλωσις τῶν Μνημείων τῆς Ἀκροπόλεως, 1940, the restoration of the monuments of the Acropolis which had taken place until the Second World War.

Many years ago a descriptive catalogue of the Museum of the Acropolis was published by the British Archaeological School at Athens. It is in two volumes, the first being a catalogue of the sculptures of the Archaic period, Catalogue of the Acropolis Museum I. Archaic Sculpture, by G. Dickins, 1912; the second by Casson is a catalogue of the sculptures of the Classical and later periods as well as architectural fragments, which includes a supplement on the clay figurines found on the Acropolis by Dorothy Brooke, date of publication 1921.

A composite picture of the antiquities of Athens and the Acropolis, extremely conscientious and complete, is given by W. Judeich in his, even now, irreplaceable book, Topographie von Athen, 1931 which constitutes volume III, 2, 2 of the series Handbuch der Altertumswissenschaft.

Worthy of special mention is O. Walter's guide to the monuments of the Acropolis, Die Akropolis von Athen, which was issued in 1929 by the Austrian Archaeological Institute of Athens as the first volume in a series of guides to Greek archaeological sites. The description of the monuments and the exposition of the issues connected with them is so strictly scientific and exhaustive that, despite the addition of data in recent years, such as the discovery of earlier stages in the cult of Athena Nike, Walter's guide-book continues to be the best one to have been written about the Acropolis.

Recently (1953) I. Th. Hill included in her book, The Ancient City of Athens, both the history and description of the monuments of the Acropolis in periods.

A simple and explicit description of the monuments of the Acropolis with good photographs and plans is contained in the Pictorial Dictionary of Ancient Athens by I. Travlos, (to whom warm thanks are due for the permission to reproduce in this book his valuable drawings), which was published in 1971 by the German Archaeological Institute of Athens in both German and English.

We repeat that a great number of books and articles about the Acropolis and its monuments has been omitted. To mention all is an impossibility even though many of them are worthwhile. The authors of the books which have been mentioned are also well-known as writers of other, specific studies on the monuments of the Acropolis. Many other archaeologists, architects etc. have dealt with the Acropolis, its monuments and dedications;

we must confine ourselves to mentioning their names only even though their works, along with those referred to above, constitute mighty stones in the foundation of our knowledge about the Acropolis : Dörpfeld, Lechat, Praschniker, Welter, Hill, Stevens, Dinsmoor, Carpenter, Berger, Harrison, Jeppesen.

Judeich's book contains the older bibliography. The more recent one from Judeich's time until 1960 is to be found in an, unfortunately difficult-to-obtain, typed script by the American St. Glass, then student at the American School of Classical Studies in Athens entitled A Bibliography of Works on Athenian Topography since Judeich. The principal bibliography concerning the Acropolis up until the present day is included in Büsing's article, Marb. Winckelmann Pr. 1969, entitled, Vermutungen über die Akropolis zu Athen, p. 1-30.

I wish to thank Mr. G. Dontas, Director of the Acropolis for making it possible for me to carry out this work, to Mr. J. Travlos, for his kind permission to reproduce his valuable plans, and Mr. D. Charisiades and Mr. S. Meletzis for the photographs which they so generously provided to me.

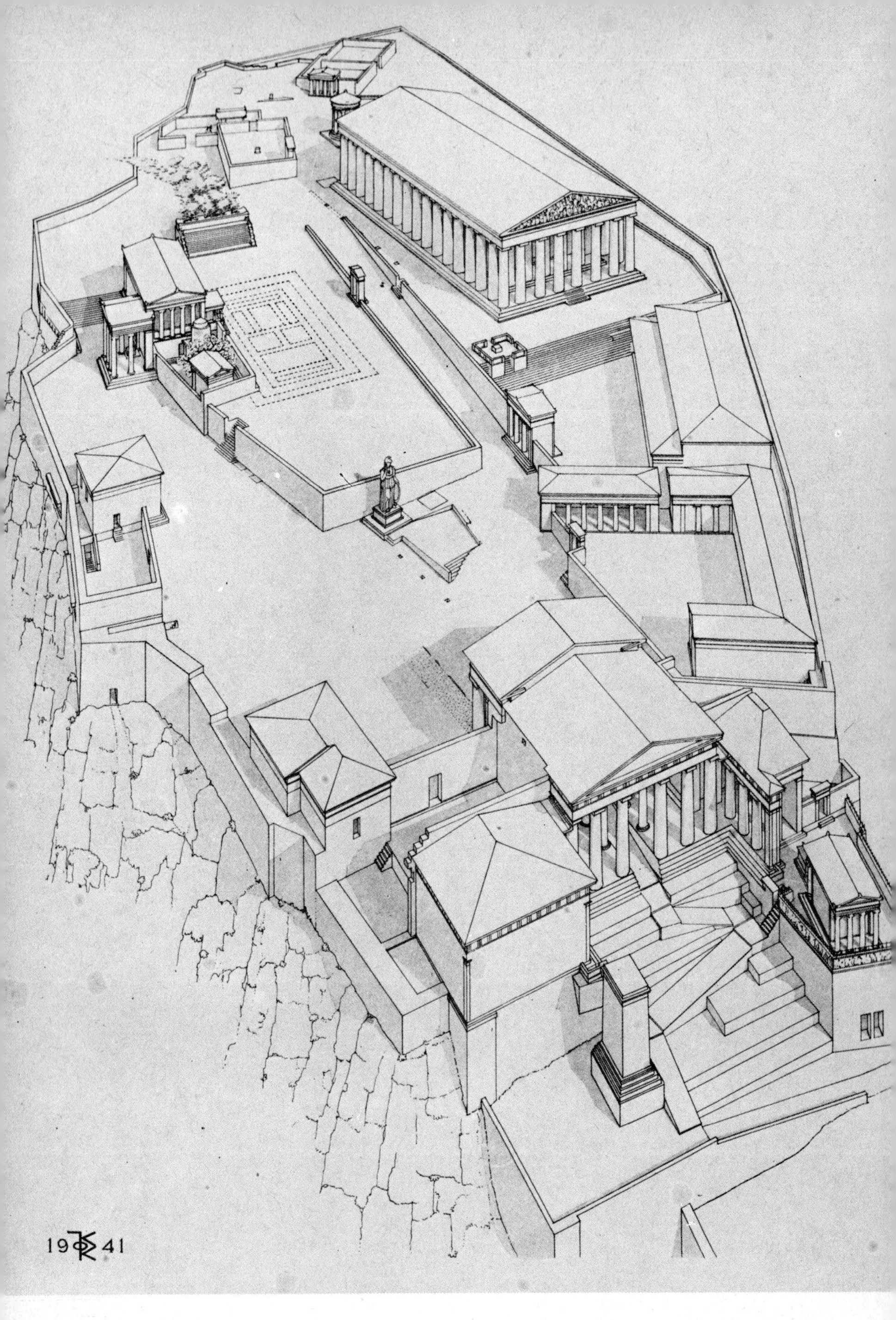

Plan 1. Reconstruction of the monuments of the Acropolis (after Stevens).

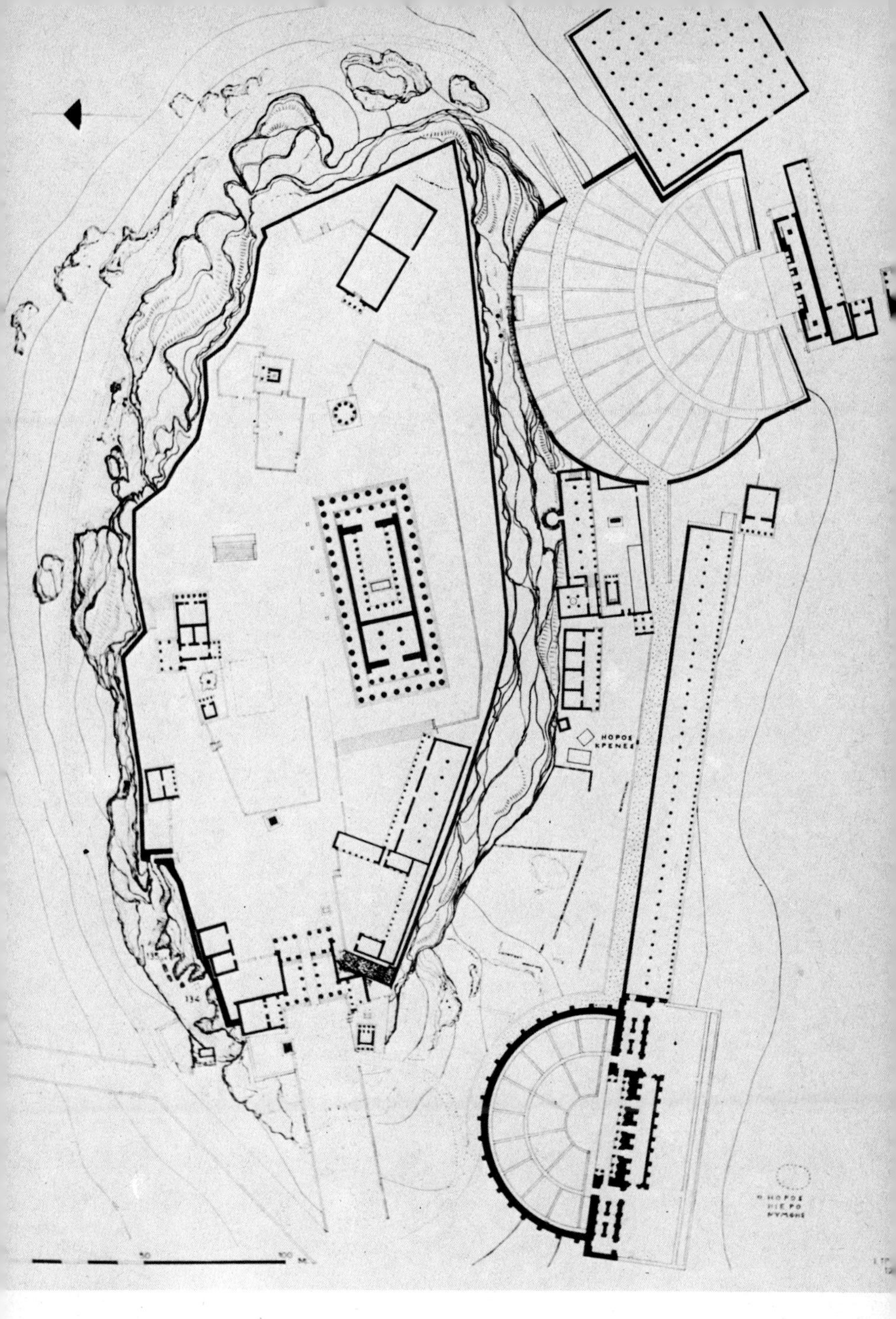

Plan 2. Plan of the Acropolis.

HISTORICAL NOTE

In very ancient times when men inhabited places, particularly hills, which for one reason or another afforded protection from the myriad dangers which menaced them, the Acropolis, one of the hills arising from the Athens basin was selected as the most suitable for human settlement (Thucydides 2, 15: *What is now the Acropolis was then the city...*). One can easily guess why prehistoric man preferred this hill to others of the region. Its natural fortification was, of course, a basic reason for its choice for the hill is rocky and sheer on all sides excepting the west one where there is a comfortable, gentle and easily defendable access. Also the fact that its upper surface was sufficiently large to accomodate a settlement, of course of the extent of that period, was an essential advantage. But perhaps the most significant reason was that there were wells of potable water which was the most necessary attribute of every fortified place.

It is very difficult for us to extricate the historical events of that distant past from the reticulum of mythical tradition of later antiquity which refers to that period. In the case of Athens however the information is so plentiful that, along the building and other remains of life, it helps us establish at least the most basic junctures in the prehistory of Athens.

The population of the Acropolis (then a simple fortress) lived under the protection of the local ruler whose Megaron was in the northern part of the rock, that is on the site where, many centuries later, the Erechtheion was built. At first the settlement on the Acropolis was nothing more than one of the many independent Attic settlements. However, as time passed, the power of the local ruler increased and his influence spread so much that at a certain — nowadays indeterminable — moment, during the so-called Mycenaean Age (2nd half of the 2nd millennium B.C.), one of the rulers, according to tradition the king Theseus, peacefully united the whole of Attica (excepting Eleusis which was conquered by the Athenians much later, perhaps in the 7th century B.C.) under the central administration of the Acropolis.

Then, or a little later, the threat of invasion obliged the Athenian king to surround the rock of the Acropolis with a very strong rampart of immense, irregular stones which in historical times was known as the Cyclopean Wall.

The Mycenaean king was not only the political leader of his state he was also its spiritual head. Within his Megaron was the official shrine of his realm, dedicated to the great fertility goddess. The cult of this goddess was, by Neolithic times already, widespread among the cultivating peoples living around the Aegean. Physical boundaries and various local factors resulted in the divinity being called by different names of which some, in the fullness of time, ended up as panhellenic. One of these was Athena (or Athenaea in older form) which means Athenian woman and is obviously derived from the name of the city.

Following the unsuccessful Dorian invasion of Attica in the 11th century B.C., the old institution of hereditary kingship was abolished, peacefully it seems. From that time the wealthy land-owners shared the authority (type of government known later as *aristocracy*, that is the state of the best). The new rulers transferred the administration to the lower city the *asty*, which constituted the kernel of the subsequent democratic state. The hill, which continued to be known until at least the 4th century B.C., as *polis*, was consecrated to the cult of Athena and other gods and for many centuries constituted the most important religious zone of the city.

Apparently in the 8th century, on the site of the old and by then completely derelict Mycenaean palace a small temple dedicated to Athena Polias, patroness of the city, was built. Homer mentions it twice, once in the Iliad (B 549) as *wealthy temple* and once in the Odyssey (κ 81) as *respected house of Erechtheus*. Within it was kept the venerable olive-wood statue of the goddess (*«xoanon»*) which was so old it was believed to have fallen from heaven (*«dhiipetes»*). The Athenians marked and revered sacred signs of divine visitations which were in the vicinity of this temple. Among these were the olive tree of Athena, the marks left by Poseidon's trident, the *Erechtheian Sea*, the Tomb of Kekrops etc. Nothing has survived from this far-off temple except two stone bases near the south wall of the Erechtheion which the Greek Archaeological Service has surrounded with railings; they were the bases of the columns of the pronaos of the temple which were evidently of wood.

During the 6th century there was much building activity on the Acropolis as in other Hellenic sanctuaries. It was then that the old temple of Athena was rebuilt, much enlarged yet still known as the *Old Temple* even though it replaced the older one. Indeed, this name was also assigned to the Erechtheion which succeeded it. Consequently, though the Persian destruction of 480 B.C. (see below) was the reason why so many architectural components from the Archaic period have survived, it is still doubtful whether the *Old Temple* was built once or twice during the 6th century and whether in the second instance it was built on both occasions to the same dimensions or first smaller and then larger. This latter opinion was formerly held; that is it was thought that the foundations of bluish Acropolis limestone which are preserved right to the south of the Erechtheion, belonged to a primary phase of the temple of the 6th century (c. 570 B.C.) which did not have a pteron; the foundations of poros-stone which surround the others were said to originate from a second phase of the same temple (c. 525 B.C.) when a pteron was added to the building by the children of Peisistratos. Nowadays this theory is outmoded and archaeologists believe that right from the beginning, in the 6th century indeed, the temple had its large dimensions irrespective of the material of its foundations. They are, nonetheless, divided over another issue; some maintain that the temple knew two constructional phases, one in the early 6th cent. B.C. and one in 525 B.C., others that the temple was built all at once in 525 B.C.

Adjacent to the *Old Temple* of Athena and to the south of it yet another temple is said to have been built in the 6th century B.C. Of lenght 100 Attic feet it would for this reason have been the *Hekatompedhos Temple;* this too dedicated to Athena but to an Athena very different from the other. While the goddess of the *Old Temple*, Polias, was guardian of the fruits of the earth, of the crops and of the fecundity, the goddess of the new temple which, like the old one was rebuilt more than once (with brilliant culmination the Parthenon) was martial, defender of the city and bore the epithet Pallas.

During the Archaic period there existed alongside these great edifices other smaller buildings, referred to as *oikemata* in the inscriptions. Some of them at least were, like the treasuries in other Hellenic sanctuaries e.g. Olympia and Delphi, buildings in which precious objects, vessels, money, etc., were stored. Although their foundations have not been found anywhere there is proof of their existence both from the inscriptions and from the formidable quantity of architectural and sculptural fragments whose dimensions are smaller than the remains of the two large temples of the Acropolis. On studying this material, archaeologists have been able to verify the existence of five *oikemata* to which in order to distinguish between them, they have applied the letters A to E. In accordance with most recent opinion, buildings C and E were located to the west of the Parthenon, building B was to the north of the Archaic Propylon on the site of the Pinakotheke of the Propylaea of Mnesicles.

In the time of Peisistratos and the Peisistratids, apart from the afore-mentioned repair or reconstruction of the *Old Temple*, the whole of the Acropolis was crowded with votives. In size and artistic merit they surpassed all earlier votives, thus making manifest the great economic and artistic acme experienced by the city in those years. There were statues of marble or bronze, vases and other objects, committed by devout and grateful Athenians to the goddess who increasingly conquered their hearts. Outstanding among them all are the so-called Korai, marble statues of women who, smiling and in star-embroidered raiment were consecrated to the goddess.

When in 490 B.C. the youthful Athenian Democracy achieved with Miltiades that brilliant military victory at Marathon, consolidating for the first time Greek courage over the fear which the Persians had hitherto provoked, it was decided, so some scholars believe, to erect a new temple to replace the old Parthenon, that is the temple of Pallas Athena who had fought so decisively and effectively on the side of the Athenians.

The new temple had risen to the height of the columns when the Persians captured the Acropolis and set fire to everything (480 B.C.). The whole brilliant and festive world of votives, magnificent temples and other buildings with their polymorphic and polychrome modelled compositions crumbled. Only a few days later Greek ships crushed the Persian fleet at Salamis and two years later, following the triumphant Greek victory at Plataeae in Boeotia, the Athenians returned to their home. But the Acropolis was by then a mound of wrecked and blackened ruins. The Athenians piously buried the majority *in situ* as if they were sacred heirlooms, infilling the cavities in the rock with them, so levelling the surface and preparing the sanctuary for its second period of splendour, the Classical.

At the same time Themistocles, triumphant at Salamis and temporary protagonist of Athenian politics after the victory, hurriedly fortified the city of Athens and the northern part of the Acropolis with ramparts which bear his name. In both instances he used the ruins of earlier monuments and other works of art as building material. The old temple of Athena was repaired so that worship could continue.

The victory at Salamis and, in particular, the founding of the anti-Persian alliance by the politician Aristides the Just distinguished Athens as foremost power in the Hellenic world.

Kimon, son of Miltiades, built the Long Walls uniting Athens with its new harbour Piraeus, in order to protect the city even more effectively from foreign incursions. Simultaneously he fortified the southern sector of the Acropolis which had remained unwalled and was later called Kimonian after him. According to some scholars, particularly of the last generation, the building of the Parthenon was only begun then and on Kimon's death in 450 B.C. it was unfinished. Only in a new design (but with many of the architectural and sculptural components from the earlier temple according to Carpenter) was it completed a few years later by Pericles.

With the aversion of the Persian menace and the, all be it temporary, peace with Sparta, the power of Athens reached its zenith. Concurrently, an unprecedented intellectual and artistic blossoming connected with the personality and name of Pericles was realised. Descendant of an old noble family but leader of the democratic faction which sought by all means the hegemony of Athens over the rest of the Hellenic world, Pericles believed that by embellishing the city with splendid new buildings the expansion and consolidation of Athenian political might would be positively reinforced. He embarked upon an enterprising building programme such as the Hellenic world had not known until then. The direction of the works, Pericles assigned to his friend Pheidias, sculptor, already well-known from a series of important works of art which had been set up in Athens and elsewhere. The economic means were ensured with the approval of the use of the resources of the treasury of the anti-Persian Alliance which in 454 was transferred from Delos to Athens.

The Periclean programme commenced in the year 447 B.C. with the construction of the Parthenon which constitutes perhaps the most significant event in the history of the Greek Classical period. Architects, sculptors, painters, turners and stone-masons responded to the appeal. They came from all corners of the Hellenic world and rushed to the task with divine inspiration. So were raised up, in remarkably short time, monuments whose artistic worth has been acknowledged as incomparable throughout the centuries which have since passed. The new temple which replaced the half-finished Parthenon surpassed in size, beauty and brilliance every precedent in Athenian architecture. Within it was housed the gold and ivory cult statue of Pallas Athena, made by Pheidias himself, glittering symbol of the new Athenian power. Works on the Parthenon lasted from 447 to 438 B.C. but were continued on its pediments until 432 B.C. The Propylaea were built between 437 and 432 B.C. A considerable number of monuments were erected at the same period in the city of Athens and on its countryside e.g. the Temple of Hephaistos (Theseion) in the Agora, the Odeion of Pericles on the south slope of the Acropolis near the Theatre of Dionysos, the Temple of Ares in the deme of Acharnae (under the reign of Augustus transferred to the Agora), one of the branches of the Long Walls etc.

The work on Propylaea was not finished yet when the Peloponnesian War, between Athens and Sparta, broke out in the year 431 B.C. The building programme of Pericles was interrupted and, for a moment, seemingly extinguished with the loss of the great visionary in 429 B.C.

The Peace of Nicias in the year 421 B.C. gave the Athenians the opportunity of resuming the programme. The miniscule Temple of Athena Nike, near the Propylaea, was built then and the construction of the Erechtheion commenced.

But, because of the catastrophic turn of the Athenian campaign in Sicily from 415 to 413 B.C., work on the Erechtheion was suspended only to be recontinued and completed in the years immediately after (410 - 407 B.C.) during the brief flash of power which preceded the final disaster in 404 B.C.

From that time until the close of antiquity no other public building was added to the Acropolis except the Temple of Rome and Augustus which was built at the end of the 1st century B.C. For centuries, however, the area continued to receive the ex-votos of the devout. Gradually they filled it densely, marking it out as the most important, if not the richest, Hellenic sanctuary in terms of works of art.

From the time of the Peace of Antalkidas onward (387 B.C.), the inscriptions use the word *Acropolis* to denote the rock instead of the word *polis* which had been employed until then. The written texts had begun using the new word slightly earlier. Even if the Acropolis was considered to be satiated with buildings, in the rest of the city buildings continued to go up for centuries until the time of the Heruli whose invasion (267 A.D.) brought about a violent and harsh end to the aspect of the ancient city.

Of these buildings we note here only the most important on the southern slope of the Acropolis. At the close of the 5th century B.C., the sanctuary of Asklepios was begun (Asklepieion) near the spring of the hero Alirrhothios (nowadays a chapel of Zoodochos Pege) in the third quarter of the 4th century B.C. when the prudent politician Lykourgos governed Athens, the Theatre of Dionysos which had already operated for two centuries in simpler form, was built of stone; at the beginning of the 2nd century B.C., with donations from Eumenes king of Pergamon, a long stoa was built along the south side of the Asklepieion to protect the spectators in the event of rain (Stoa of Eumenes); finally, in the year 161 A.D. an extremely wealthy Athenian, Herodus Atticus, built the Odeion which bears his name to this day, in memory of his wife Regilla. It is still used for the performance of musical and dramatic entertainment (it was partially restored after the Second World War).

Throughout the Roman period the Acropolis kept, virtually intact, the appearance it had in the years of its acme. The majority of its votives were preserved, quite the opposite of many Greek sanctuaries which were denuded of their artistic fortunes in order to embellish public buildings in Rome, the capital of the World, or the villas of her mighty generals and officials.

With the spread of Christianity the desolation began here also. One by one, or all at once, the idolatrous works of art were transferred to Constantinople or fell victim to Christian fanaticism. The rock was rapidly bereft of its artistic wealth while some of the smaller buildings were destroyed.

But the larger ones remained to serve the new religion. The Parthenon was transformed into a church dedicated to Aghia Sophia, later to the Virgin of Athens (Panaghia the Atheniotissa). Its east entrance was closed so that the apse of the altar could be built there; thus a part of the sculpture on the east pediment was destroyed. The faithful now entered from the west side as the convention of the new religion demanded. At the same time or slightly later the Erechtheion was converted into a church dedicated to the Mother of God (Theometor) while the south wing of the Propylaea was converted into a church of the Holy Trinity (Aghia Triadha) (Pl. 2).

The last metropolitan of Athens Michael Akominatos had his palace in the Propylaea. One morning, however, in 1205, on learning that the Franks had flooded the land he handed over the Acropolis without resistance and he himself left.

From 1205 to 1456 (when it was captured by the Turks), the Acropolis passed successively from the occupation of the Franks (Dukes De la Roche) to the occupation of the Catalans and from them to the occupation of the Florentine merchants Acciajuoli of whom the last one was obliged, after a two year siege, to surrender the Acropolis to the Turks of Turahan Omar. During this period the Acropolis had been once again transformed into a fortress as it was in prehistoric times. The Parthenon had become a Catholic church dedicated to Santa Maria di Atene, the Propylaea the Grandee's palace where the Latin sovereign was installed and, on the southern section of the Propylaea old engravings show that a tall square tower had been built for the reconnaissance of the surrounding region (it was demolished 100 years ago) (Pl. 77).

During the years of the Turkish occupation the appearance of the Acropolis changed. Huge embankments entirely covered the south and west side of the hill. Old engravings of this period show only the upper part of the columns of the Propylaea; the Theatre of Dionysos and the Odeion of Herodus Atticus had vanished beneath a very thick earth mantle. The Acropolis was not considered to be an important fortress, it was not for example equivalent to Nauplion or Chalkis and was only administered by a dhisdhare. A whole village of Turkish families was established among the monuments (Pl. 3).

Until the year 1656 the most important monuments on the Acropolis remained almost intact. This is clearly shown us by the sketches left by European travellers who began to reach Greece (for instance Spon and Wheler) in these times. In that year, on the eve of the feast of Saint Demetrios, a thunderbolt struck the Propylaea, which had been converted into a powder magazine, and they were blown sky high.

Next was the turn of the Nike Temple. In the face of the Venetian threat of Morosini to the Acropolis in 1687, the Turks pulled it down and utilised its parts as building material for a fortification wall with which they fenced off the entrance to the Acropolis between the Nike Bastion and the Pinakotheke. In engravings of 1751 and 1765 the Nike Temple no longer appears.

The Parthenon was destroyed in 1687. The building is usually believed to have been transformed into a mosque since the very beginning of Turkish rule. According to another point of view, however, it became a mosque only after its destruction because prior to this its use as such must have been precluded by the many human representations which decorated the building and which Islam expressly forbids. In 1687 when Morosini, head of the impressive Venetian and mercenary army, captured Athens and besieged the Turks on the Acropolis, the Parthenon was used as a powder magazine. Thus one of the shells from Morosini's artillery, which bombarded the Acropolis from the opposite, hill of Philopappos fell on the Parthenon and blew it up, destroying and scattering a considerable part of its sculpted decoration. This shocking event, which is depicted in contemporary engravings, forced the commander of the castle Ali Aga to abandon his stubborn resistance and surrender. Morosini only held the Acropolis and Athens for a few months. During this time he attempted to detach part of the statues which had remained in position on the Parthenon. Some of these fell during operations and were shattered. It is not known exactly when the Turks returned to Athens. An inscription bearing the date 1708 carved on a marble of the Erechtheion mentions that a voevoda of Athens, Mustapha ephendi fixed up a new vaulted gate on the Acropolis (N.B. In this inscription one can just as easily read the year 1808). Anyway, from then until the Greek Revolution the Acropolis was nothing more than an unimportant castle.

Until the 18th century the Erechtheion was used as the residence of the dhisdhare. Then the commander of the Acropolis built a new residence between the Parthenon and the Erechtheion.

By the 18th century travellers visited the Acropolis more frequently. On leaving they all took with them some little work of art as a souvenir of their presence. The greatest and most systematic theft of works of art took place a few years before the Greek Revolution by the British ambassador to Constantinople, Lord Elgin. Supplied with special permission from the sultan and with the aid of the Neapolitan sculptor Lusieri he removed within a few years the greater part of the sculpted decoration of the Parthenon which had escaped the destruction of 1687 and the attempts of Morosini, plus one of the Karyatides and other antiquities. Elgin's action did not pass without provoking strong reaction in England itself, from Lord Byron for example. But when

Elgin's collections was sold to the British Museum, of which to this day it constitutes one of the most famous and impressive assemblages in the world (Elgin Marbles), the satisfaction which the acquisition of such a precious fortune evoked, prevailed over the romantic objections.

In June 1822 Odysseus Androutsos captured the Acropolis after a siege and installed Gouras as its chief sentinel. Some years later, in 1826, the Greeks were besieged in their turn by the troops of Kutachee and after a heŕoic defence surrendered in 1827. The Acropolis did not return to the Greeks until several years later, after the termination of the struggle for Independence in 1833.

Following the liberation of Greece and the creation of an independent state the first task of the authorities was to clear away the ruins of the Turkish settlement. The reestablishment of the ancient monuments was also begun. Ross reassembled the Nike Temple in position. Between 1885 and 1890 excavations were carried out over the whole area of the Acropolis and revealed the incredible artistic treasures of the Archaic period. From 1900 onwards the systematic restoration of the monuments commenced. The Propylaea were restored between 1909 and 1917, the Erechtheion from 1902 to 1908, the Parthenon from 1898 to 1900 and from 1922 to 1933. Finally the Nike Temple was restored for a second time, together with its tower this time, just before the Second World War.

After the Second World War restoration condinued on a very minor scale. No less important, we believe, is the conservation of the monuments which has been the declared aim of the Greek Archaeological Service in recent years.The attempt, that is, to check the destruction wrought by rain, frost, air pollution and many other dangers and to preserve, at least as they appear today, these most beautiful monuments of antiquity.

THE PREHISTORIC ACROPOLIS

So splendid and impressive are the monuments of the Classical period on the Acropolis that the prehistoric remains pass virtually unnoticed by many.

As has been said already, the rock of the Acropolis and its environs have a very long history. Pottery found both on the rock itself and on its slopes has demonstrated that men have lived here at least since the Neolithic period. The principal and oldest «mass» Neolithic find was discovered outside the north-west corner of the rock near the Klepsydra spring, where 22 shallow wells full of Neolithic pottery were revealed. Also on the southern slopes of the Acropolis, in 1922, ruins of many houses of the Neolithic period as well as pottery were found. The same spots produced pottery of the Early Bronze Age. But a gap is observed at the end of this period. The so-called Middle Helladic period (2000 to 1600 B.C.) is again represented by an abundance of pottery of excellent quality. During this period the first Greeks were settling in the Helladic area, subjugating or expelling (as in the case of Athens) the mysterious Pelasgians.

In the so-called Late Helladic IIIB period (1300 to 1200 B.C.) the Acropolis, which had meanwhile become an important settlement, was still unwalled. Perhaps to this period belongs a series of retaining walls (the remains are negligible) in the central and northern area of the Acropolis; these circumvented the palace of the local ruler, of which too very little remains (see below). This complex of retaining walls occupied precisely the area between the Erechtheion and the Parthenon which later developed into the pre-eminent place of worship with important shrines and minor buildings. Access at that time was through two entrances, a west one situated somewhere near the Propylaea and a north-east one which passed between the rocks to the north-east of the subsequent Erechtheion (nowadays visible thanks to a special wall built by the Archaeological Service). These have almost completely disappeared because the area was intensively built upon in later years and their existence has only been confirmed thanks to the meticulous investigations of specialists. From the palace proper nothing has remained except one column base of limestone and two steps of sandstone which nowadays rest upon the northern rampart of the Acropolis (Pl. 4a), directly north-east of the Erechtheion. Almost none of the walls found in excavations correspond with certainty to the walls of the palace.

It is, however, certain that during the final phase of the Late Helladic IIIB period considerable building activity took place on the Acropolis. The incursions of marauding tribes (Dorians? Illyrians?) forced the king of the Acropolis to surround it with a mighty rampart as much as 6 m. thick in places. It was made of irregular blocks of stone on both faces and the interstices and spaces between the two faces were infilled with smaller stones. This work, monumental and imposing, was attributed by the Greeks of Classical times to the Cyclops, beings with supernatural strength (Cyclopean) (see also chapter on the Fortification Wall).

Similar wall constructions are known from other Mycenaean acropoles such as Mycenae, Tiryns and Gla. The wall on the Athenian Acropolis is so well-made as to permit the suggestion that it is due to the same masons who, at that time, travelled around to different places in order to help, with their superior craftsmanship, in the effectual defence against the predatory raiders who then scourged Greece. The largest section of the Mycenaean rampart of the Acropolis is that which is preserved to the east of the Nike Temple and extends southwards from the corner of the south wing of the Propylaea towards the Classical Wall (Pl. 5). Nearby was the entrance to the Mycenaean Acropolis (see above) as well as a mighty tower which protected its southern side (remains in the interior of the Classical Nike Bastion, a visit being possible by permission of the Director of the Acropolis). These are not, however, the sole sections of the Mycenaean rampart which have survived. Others of significance are: a section discernible at the bottom of a trench southwest of the Parthenon (Pl. 6), another in the basement of the Museum, a third visible behind the north-east façade of the Museum, very near the former (Pl. 4b). The course of the rampart is more or less well-known thanks to these sections as well as to the assiduous study of traces of its placement on the rock. In general the Mycenaean wall seems to have followed the brow of the rock. In the southern part of the Acropolis it passed much further inside the line of the Classical rampart which made use of huge infillings aimed at enlarging the sanctuary for the construction of the Parthenon (see below).

Within the Mycenaean stronghold was a spring which was on the northern flank of the rock at the bottom of a schism in the rock. It was excavated shortly before the Second World War by the American archaeologist Broneer.

Just as on other Mycenaean acropoles there existed a second minor fortress lower down than the main one (German «Unterburg») north-west of the rock. Its construction was necessary for security reasons because it encompassed the region of caves which were potentially very dangerous if they fell into enemy hands. According to Iakovidhes, to whom we mainly owe the confirmation of the existence of a second, lower rampart, this is the «Pelargic» repeatedly referred to in the ancient sources. Much later, in the difficult days of the Peloponnesian War, the Pelargic was used for the settlement of refugees who, despite the Delphic oracle which prophesied that *better the Pelargic be left empty* selected stones from the remains of the rampart to found altars. According to Iakovidhes, in Classical times the Pelargic was taken for the Enneapylon, a complex of walls and accesses to the south-west and west of the Acropolis built in Geometric and Archaic times.

THE ACCESS TO THE ACROPOLIS

Since earliest times the entrance to the Acropolis has been from its west side which is the only one where the ground is more or less easy (for the northern Mycenaean entrance see chapter on the Prehistoric Acropolis). During Mycenaean times a simple, narrow pathway wended its way from the south of the rock and, skirting the base of the mighty bastion, later to become the Nike Bastion, mounted the western slope in double zig-zag line and terminated at the fortified entrance located on the site of the present-day south wing of the Propylaea. Deep cuttings still preserved on the rock surface at the foot of the Nike Bastion originate from that very ancient pathway and attest its route (Pl. 7a).

The need to create a second, more comfortable access directly from the west was soon felt. This need must have arisen after the transfer of the political centre of Athens, from the Acropolis to the lower city and in particular to the Agora which was to the north of the rock. It became imperative when, shortly before the middle of the 6th century B.C. (566 B.C.) the Panathenaic festival was reorganised and it was necessary to facilitate the movement of an enormous crowd of believers. A ramp, approximately 80 m. long by 10 m. wide, was made then. It led directly from the western foothills of the Acropolis up until the entrance which was modelled at that time (see below). Many sections of the northern retaining wall of this monumental access are preserved. It is built of polygonal masonry according to the system of the period. The most significant of these sections is to be found directly east of the Beulé Gate (Pl. 7b).

This access remained unaltered until the days of Pericles. When Mnesicles built the Propylaea he also included in his design the widening of the Archaic access to the width determined by the two projecting wings of his magnificent building. Thus the width of the old access was effectively doubled though not its length, and there also was a retaining wall on its northern side. A noteworthy section preserved between the Pedestal of Agrippa and the north bastion of the Beulé Gate is composed of large poros-blocks laid isodomically but placed obliquely as the incline dictated (Pl. 8a). Correspondingly, the south side of the rock which is here preserved at a much higher level is hewn vertically towards the access side. Its upper surface also slopes (Pl. 8b) indicating that the poros stone blocks rested upon it just as on the northern retaining branch. It is uncertain how the slope was arranged internally and what the older Archaic surface was like.

In the time of the emperor Claudius (52 A.D.) a monumental staircase replaced the access of the Classical period without, however, abolishing the lateral retaining walls which, on the contrary, were also utilised for the new staircase (Pl. 8b). The work was in keeping with the theatrical taste of the Imperial Roman era and included a middle section in which the steps are closer together to facilitate the ascent. Pieces of this staircase (Pl. 9a - b) were used by the archaeologist Pittakes in the years just after the liberation of Greece to reestablish a part of the staircase which for many years was used by visitors to the Acropolis. In 1959 the Beulé Gate was abolished and the very ancient pathway coming from the south-west was used for the access, the major part of the staircase was removed in order to further emphasise the picturesque elements of the entrance rather than the «Classicising» ones hitherto exalted. A few years later, in 1968, the Beulé Gate was reopened to visitors. So far the reinstating of Pittakes' staircase (of which only the lower part has been kept) has not taken place.

A poros-stone altar in the cavity east of the Beulé Gate,

near to the polygonal wall (P l. 10) was most probably used though no inscription remains, for sacrifices to Apollo Agyieus, patron of highways and entrances. Another inscription of the Imperial era which was found nearby records that the gate keeper of the Acropolis dedicated an altar to this deity.

In the 3rd century A.D., probably after the catastrophic invasion of the Heruli in 267 A.D., the entire area west of the Propylaea was enclosed as a fortress with two gateways, one to the west and one below the Nike Bastion The western gate (nowadays called the Beulé Gate after the French archaeologist who excavated it in 1852) was flanked by two bastions (the north one has been restored and is now used as a ticket office). From a casual glance it is clear that the building material of the gate and the bastions consists of architectural members and inscriptions of earlier times. A significant proportion are architectural components from the Choregic monument of Nicias which was located near the Theatre of Dionysos (between it and the Stoa of Eumenes, where its foundations still remain).

From that time on and throughout the Medieval and Turkish occupation, the Acropolis became a fortress once again.

THE MONUMENT OF AGRIPPA

West of the north wing of the Propylaea and parallel with the foundation of the Pinakotheke stands a tall pedestal known as the Monument or Pedestal of Agrippa (Pl. 11).

This pedestal consists of a rectangular foundation (3.31 × 3.80 m.) which is 4.50 m. high and is surmounted by a main body 8.91 m. high which tapers slightly towards the top. The latter is of bluish Hymettan marble except for its (projected) cornice and base which are of white Pentelic marble. The foundation is of conglomerate and poros-stone. The main body of the pedestal is built according to the so-called pseudo-isodomic technique particularly beloved in Hellenistic times The surface bore, as the traces testify, a bronze four-horse chariot. The following inscription is preserved on the west face of the pedestal:

The demos (offered) to Marcus Agrippa son of Lucius, thrice Consul.

This witnesses that the charioteer was the son-in-law of the Roman emperor Augustus, Marcus Agrippa, who was famous for his pro-Athenian sentiments. The architecture of the monument is, however, older than the Roman period. It is reminiscent of similar pedestals set up in Delphi by the kings of Pergamon Attalos I and Eumenes II, by the king of Bithynia Prussias, by the Roman general Aemilius Paulus (after his victory at Pydna) and by the Rhodians (chariot of Helios) and those in other Greek sanctuaries. Beneath the inscription of Agrippa are faintly discernible the traces of another earlier inscription. It is now believed that the base was originally erected by Eumenes II, king of Pergamon (197 - 158 B.C.) following his victory in the

Panathenaic Games of 178 B.C. and that it bore a four-horse chariot the drivers of which were himself and his brother Attalos. This chariot was replaced by that of Agrippa probably around 27 B.C.

PROPYLAEA

The word propylaea, like the word propylon, means the monumental arrangement of a gateway either of some sacred place or city, or agora etc. This arrangement can be elementary, for example a plain roofed space with two passages, one leading towards the inside of the sanctuary and one towards the outside. Usually, however, it is an edifice with architectural claims. The Propylaea of the Acropolis belong to this second category and without exaggeration may be considered as the most monumental example bequeathed us by the Antiquity (Pl. 12).

In Late Archaic times there was a less monumental Propylon at the entrance to the Acropolis. It was destroyed by the Persians in 480 B.C. along with the other buildings on the rock but was in all probability repaired later and used until the time of Pericles. A part of that Propylon is still preserved to an appreciable height behind the south wall of the Periclean Propylaea (Pl. 14, 15a-b) evidently because, for some reason or other unknown to us, Mnesicles did not wish to demolish it, just as he did not pull down the adjacent section of the Cyclopean (Mycenaean) fortification wall. Apart from this portion, the presence of the Late Archaic Propylon is also attested by the cuttings in the rock on the central axis of the Periclean Propylaea which represent the beds for the foundations of the building. Thanks to the careful study of all these details, the reconstruction of the original form of the Late Archaic Propylon has been made possible. Its axis was not east-west as in the Propylaea of Pericles but north-east - south-west. It was also smaller and, furthermore, did not have wings like its successor. Both its façades had four columns between

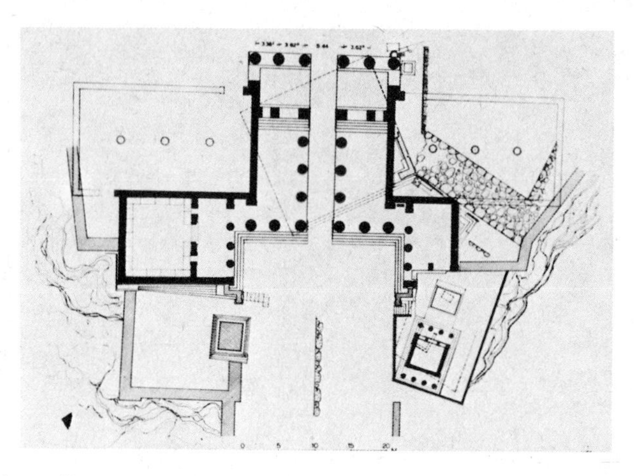

Plan 3

door jambs and there were probably five portals as in the Periclean Propylaea. Finally, on its west façade and along the west side of the Cyclopean Wall was a step-like platform probably used as a rest place (Plan 3; Pl. 14).

The good preservation of the Late Archaic Propylon (see the extant section) witnesses clearly that it had only recently been erected when it was destroyed. The most likely period of its construction is during the decade after the Battle of Marathon, if not immediately after the Persians as is recently postulated. Certainly it belonged to the same building programme that included the construction of the Parthenon. It seems improbable however that the Acropolis retained until this period the plain old Mycenaean entrance. Thus we must speculate that when the great Panathenaea were organized in 566 B.C. and the large access previously discussed was built, a Propylon worthy of receiving the faithful who accompanied the goddess' peplos was also built. Here then there has been a succession of edifices roughly corresponding to the succession of buildings of the *Old Temple* and the Parthenon: Propylaea I 566 B.C.; Propylaea II, after the Battle of Marathon; (when not after 480 B.C.); Propylaea III, time of Pericles.

If the basic purpose of the Propylon of any sanctuary was the spiritual preparation of the pilgrim for the spectacle of the temple and votives which would confront him, in other words to link the sanctuary with the world outside, the sacred with the profane, then the architect of the Propylaea sought solely to impress with the monumental character which he imparted to the building. The architect Mnesicles, one of the close collaborators of Pericles and Pheidias, evidently wanted to endow his work with the same breadth as Iktinos and Kallikrates had given to the Parthenon. We are informed by the ancient sources that the building was put up in the years intervening between the completion of the Parthenon and the outbreak of the Peloponnesian War, that is from 437 to 432 B.C., at a cost of 2012 talents. The tool marks visible on the bases of many columns (Pl. 16a), the bosses left on many stones mainly on the north-east external wall (Pl. 19), the half-worked surfaces in the alcoves between the central building and the lateral constructions (Pl. 16b) clearly testify that the building remained half-finished, probably because of the imminent war. Even though an attempt was later made to complete the work, during the interval of the Peace of Nicias, it was never finished, perhaps because the outlay was not considered essential or even because, over the years, the elements which remained unworked were thought to be decorative.

The Propylaea are comprised of a central building and two lower wings (Pl. 12). The former is rectangular (24 × 18.20 m.) with a west-east axis. In front of its west façade is a row of six Doric columns aligned from north to south. They are placed at regular intervals (intercolumniations) except for the two middle ones between which an unusually large aperture has been left, intended to facilitate the movement of the pilgrims and sacrificial animals to the shrine. Perpendicular to these columns, on the inside of the building, two rows of three tall Ionic columns supported the roof. These divided the space lengthwise into three sections.

Behind this central building a second eastern section was situated at a higher level. Communication between the sections was through five portals, a large central one, two smaller ones to right and left and two yet smaller ones at the extremities. These doorways, which narrowed towards the top, had heavy wooden doors which closed by themselves when opened (the present-day marble investments are from the Imperial period). In front of the eastern section of the central building there is a row of six Doric columns facing the sanctuary (Pl. 13). Both sections of the central building had separate pedimented roofs and a dentelated sima of which a part is preserved upon the building, on the northern side of the eastern section (Pl. 18). The roof of the central building was coffered (a portion has been restored) and these were formerly painted with golden stars on a deep blue background (Pl. 17). The stylobate all around and the steps leading to the eastern section are of ash-grey Eleusinian marble. Of the same marble is a type of bench which originally ran along the entire length of the north and south wall of the central building. The central building was imitated by the Athenians in the 2nd century A.D. in the Great Propylaea of Eleusis.

The façade of the north-west wing consisted of three Doric columns between two door jambs creating a stoa like a vestibule in front of a chamber (10.76 × 8.97 m.) which one enters via a doorway placed off the axis. On both sides of the doorway, asymmetrically placed, are windows. This chamber is called the Pinakotheke because it was used for the exhibition of paintings (Pausanias simply calls it *a building with pictures*). It is neither testified nor verified whether these works were pictures or murals, just as the wall has no signs of holes which would advocate the first view, neither have been preserved paint marks which would certify the second. It is, of course, not impossible for the stucco to have vanished with the passage of time, or for the murals to have been made without the use of plaster. Pausanias mainly cites the works of anonymous artists excepting «Achilles in Skyros» which he tells us was made by the famous artist Polygnotus of Thasos, who lived in the middle of the 5th century B.C. This chamber was apparently also a place where visitors could relax, something like a «Lounge» (Lesche) such as we often come across in Greek sanctuaries (c.f. the Lesche of the Knidians at Delphi). In this case couches were placed all around the walls (Plan 4) and for this reason (not aesthetic) the portal of the Pinakotheke is placed off the axis.

To maintain symmetry another corresponding wing existed to the south-west of the main building. This was much smaller than the north-west one (8.97 × 5.23 m.), consisting of a vestibule similar to that of its counterpart though slightly deeper and without a chamber. It does not have a west wall either, in its place is a door jamp. These deviations from symmetry are evidently due to the architect's desire to respect the adjoining sections of the old Cyclopean Wall (Pl. 5) and the Sanctuary of Brauronian Artemis which was preserved towards the south, as well as the Shrine of Athena Nike to the south-west to which, otherwise, every road of approach would be cut off. According to older theories there was some retrenchment of the initial design on the inside of the Propylaea as well, that is the side facing the sanctuary. Some scholars believed that here Mnesicles intended to add two more stoas, one to the right and one to the left of the

Plan 4

central building. As evidence they cite the existence of two door jambs next to the eastern ones on the walls of the central building, that on the north wall facing north, the one on the south wall, south. Their existence would not have been necessary unless Mnesicles had in mind the extension of the building with stoas on these sides (Pl. 19).

In the 1st century A.D. a monumental staircase was built in front of the Propylaea (see chapter on the Access). It occupied the entire width of the access and was partially restored during the 19th century (Pl. 9a-b) but removed a few years ago in order to make the paved street along which visitors to the Acropolis pass today. With the building of this monumental staircase the entrance to the great Athenian sanctuary was even further emphasised in a manner befittingly theatrical.

Finally, to the east of the Pinakotheke a reservoir for the collection of rain-water was built.

In Early Christian times the south wing of the Propylaea was converted into a church. Preserved on the floor in front of the eastern wall are the traces of the supports of the altar table. Later, in the 10th century, another church dedicated to the Taxiarchs was founded on the axis of the Propylaea. Traces of wall-paintings of the Archangels Michael and Gabriel were preserved on either side of the central entrance.

Throughout the years of Frankish rule the governors had their residence here, indeed they transformed the north wing into a two-storey building. Holes in the walls result from this conversion and were used to receive the beams for the floor. The three windows on the east wall were also opened at that time (Pl. 20). A chapel dedicated to Saint Bartholomew was founded within the palace. Travlos associates with this the ruins of a third church found to the north of the Propylaea, behind the Pinakotheke (AE 1853, p. 939; Beulé, L'Acropole d'Athènes, pl. 2; Travlos, Πολεοδομική 'Εξέλιξις τῶν 'Αθηνῶν, p. 138, note 5).

The most important addition to the Propylaea was the Koulas, a high rectangular tower attached to their southern wing, which enabled the control of an extensive area around the Acropolis (it is depicted in old engravings and was demolished in 1874).

During the years of Turkish occupation, the Propylaea were used as a powder magazine for some time. Consequently, when lightning struck the building in 1645 it caused immense destruction. In 1687 the Turks reinforced the defences of the Acropolis in the face of Morosini's imminent attack, by fencing off the Propylaea with a fortification wall mainly consisting of pieces from the Nike Temple.

After the liberation of Greece, the rampart was pulled down and the Propylaea released from its suffocating embrace.

Restoration works were begun by Balanos in 1909 and completed by Prof. Orlandos in 1963.

TEMPLE OF ATHENA NIKE

On the bastion which seemingly projects so abruptly to the west of the rock of the Acropolis stands the tiny Temple of Athena Nike (Pl. 22 - 23). A refreshing note in the heroic symphony of the Propylaea, a smile in their restrained sobriety, it nonetheless blends in with them without dissonance. Most elegant in its small dimensions, it seems to hover in the light (Pl. 22).

The history of this area does not begin with the temple we behold today. When works were carried out for the support of the bastion and temple shortly before the Second World War, it was discovered, with the demolition of the Classical bastion that the Classical temple was but the end product of a centuries-long history.

In the Mycenaean period the projection of the rock was fortified with the so-called Cyclopean Wall thus forming a mighty bastion which protected the gateway to the Acropolis. This gateway was located where the south wing of the Propylaea stands, while the adjoining section of the Cyclopean Wall to the south protected its southern side. To the same period belongs a small sanctuary in the form of a double alcove. It was found after the disintegration of the bastion on its west flank, behind the alcove of the Classical period (which was kept visible after the reconstruction of the bastion Pl. 26). In that shrine the visitors left, before they had even set foot on the Acropolis, their votives to Athena who protected the rock (Lykophron names Athena Pylatis, see Charitonides, Ath. Mitt. 1960, p. 1 - 3).

In the second quarter of the 6th century B.C., if not before, the cult of Athena was transferred to the surface of the bastion. On excavating its interior the following were found 1.40 m. below the Classical surface: a) Remains of a miniscule temple in the form of a simple square building (side 3.50 m.) and an altar for burnt offerings which was full of figurines (Archaic times?) (Pl. 27). b) A poros-stone altar in front of it bearing the following inscription in characters of the middle of the 6th century B.C. *Of Athena Nike the altar, Patrokles made it.* c) A second altar of poros-stone. d) A base (the area can be visited by permission of the Director of the Acropolis through the trap-door in front of the Classical temple). The way in which the stones are worked and fit together recalls the exceptional masonry of the architectural members of the *Old Temple* (or the primordial Parthenon) and helps, in conjuction with the lettering of the inscription, to date the works. Indeed, some scholars believe that Panathenaic amphorae, which first appeared at that time, depict the Archaic statue of Athena Nike although this type does not correspond with that of the cult statue of Classical times, that is at least as Herodotus describes it (see below).

The final constructional phase of the bastion is represented by the temple and bastion of Classical times. The architect of the Classical temple was Kallikrates who was also an architect of the Parthenon. A decree of the year 448 B.C. (IG I^2 24) ordered *a door to be put on the shrine according to Kallikrates* instructions and further *a temple and an altar of stone shall be built according to a programme to be submitted by Kallikrates.* Nonetheless, there are many indications that works actually commenced much later, probably during the interval of the Peace of Nicias (421 B.C.) while the parapet surrounding the bastion was made even later about 410 B.C.

The temple is of Ionic order, amphiprostyle, with a row of four lofty thin columns 4.066 m. high in front of both its narrow faces. The epistyle resting upon these columns is divided into three, as is usual in the Ionic order. The frieze above the epistyle bore relief representations. It is mainly the eastern frieze that is still in position (Pl. 24 - 25). The other frieze sections are in the British Museum (on the building they have been replaced with casts). The eastern frieze depicts a company of gods around the enthroned Zeus. On the other sides are illustrated battles between Greeks and barbarians and Greeks against Greeks. Holes preserved on the surface of the horizontal cornices indicate that the pediments must also have been decorated with sculpted scenes. None of the figures in the Acropolis Museum, however, can now be ascribed with certainty to the sculpted decoration of the pediments, the subject of which is consequently unknown. The entrance to the temple was through a door flanked by two pillars which were connected to the side walls with railings (balustrade) perhaps to ensure that the interior of the temple had sufficient light which would otherwise have been limited due to the neighbouring south-west wing of the Propylaea. In the 3rd century B.C. pictures showing the victory of Antigonos Gonatas, king of Macedonia, over the Galatians were hung on the walls of the temple.

According to philological testimonies the cult statue of Athena Nike was wooden and represented the goddess with a pomegranate in her right hand and a helmet in the left one (Heliodorus): *The wooden statue* (*xoanon*) *of Athena was wingless with a pomegranate in her right hand and a helmet in the left.* Thus were united the two aspects of the goddess, the pacific and the polemic. Pausanias, describing the Nike Bastion, says simply that *on the right of the gateway is a temple of Wingless Victory* (*Nike*) and this name has remained in popular usage right up until the present day. In Pausanias' time it had evidently been forgotten that Nike was one of the aspects of Athena and a tradition circulated, to which Pausanias refers in another instance (III, 15, 7), that the cult statue in the temple had been represented without wings so that it could not fly away and would so stay with the Athenians forever.

The altar was situated in front of the temple. During the Panathenaic festival (IG II² 334 of the year 335/4 B.C.) *a heifer chosen from the most beautiful* was sacrificed to the goddess. Some pieces of the plaques which formed the altar have been preserved and are today arranged in one corner of the bastion.

The bastion is trapezoidal in plan. At a distance of 9.14 m. from the north-west corner, eastwards, it turns ninety degrees towards the south to form the wall of a small staircase of which only the upper part is preserved. A marble breastwork 1.05 m. high girdled the brow of the bastion on three sides, the southern, western and northern, as well as the upper part of the afore-mentioned staircase. The outer surface of the breastwork bore relief representations: Winged Victories offering sacrifices or embellishing a trophy and lithe figures of Athena. Here Nike is separate from Athena. The themes are repeated with variations on all the plaques comprising the breastwork. Most of these are exhibited in the Acropolis Museum (Gallery VIII) while a host of fragments are to be found in its store-rooms. The sculptures of the breastwork are ranked among the best works of the late 5th century B.C., exceptional examples of the skill, imagination and finesse which characterised the craftsmanship of the artists of this era. (One of the most famous sculptors of this period Kallimachos, known by the revealing epithet *Katatexitechnos*, seems to have been the principal sculptor of the breastwork of the Nike Bastion). Holes preserved at intervals on the upper surface of the breastwork make clear that this also bore a metal trellis.

Near the south side of the temple stood two statues; one of Athena Nike which was erected in memory of the victory of the Athenians over the Ambracians in 425 B.C. and a bronze one which was put up in the same year following the Athenian victory over the Lacedaemonians at Sphakteria.

From the Nike Bastion as Pausanias says, *the sea is visible*, that is it could only be surveyed from here because the high walls which formerly surrounded the rest of the rock of the Acropolis prevented one from seeing without.

He adds that Aigeus king of Athens fell to his death from the bastion in olden times because, on distinguishing from afar the ship of his son Theseus returning from Crete with black sails, he thought him dead.

A few metres east of the temple an impressive section of the Cyclopean (Mycenaean) Wall is visible.

Nearby and adjoining the south face of the Propylaea, the Austrian archaeologist Welter discovered the south-east corner of a rectangular area where Artemis was worshipped as Hekate Epipyrgidia (i.e. upon the bastion) or Phosphoros (Light Bearer). Alkamenes, the best-known sculptor and pupil of Pheidias, erected a statue of the goddess here which represented her in three aspects: as goddess of heaven, of earth and of the under-world. Thus it seems that he was the originator of a type which predominated in ensuing centuries in representations of the goddess.

The Nike Temple survived until 1687 A.D. In that year, which also proved fateful for the Parthenon, the Turks, wanting to augment the defence of the Acropolis during the supervening campaign of Morosini, pulled down the Nike Temple and used its marble to reinforce the strong fortification wall (Pl. 77) which they built between the Nike Bastion and the Pinakotheke of the Propylaea.

With the founding of the modern Greek state the reestablishment of the ruins of the Acropolis began. The architectural members and sculpted decoration of the Nike Temple and Bastion were discovered and identified. The Germans Ross and Schaubert and the Dane Hansen reconstructed the temple. However, a few years before the Second World War the tottering condition of the bastion forced the Greek Archaeological Service to pull down both it and the temple and to proceed anew with their reconstruction. On that opportunity the interior of the bastion was excavated and the principal stages of its former history revealed.

SANCTUARY OF BRAURONIAN ARTEMIS

In the days of the tyrant Peisistratos who hailed from Brauron, a demos on the eastern coast of Attica, a sanctuary dedicated to the Brauronian Artemis, patron of pregnant women and women in child-birth, was founded on the Acropolis. Principal site of the worship of the goddess, as her name indicates, was Brauron where, according to tradition, Iphigenia had brought the wooden idol of the goddess from the Tauris peninsula. The sanctuary at Brauron was excavated in the post-war years by the Ephor of Antiquities I. Papadimitriou and produced some very interesting architectural remains and finds. The shrine on the Acropolis which was, so to speak, a branch of it had been dug during the last century.

The Athenian sanctuary of Brauronian Artemis was in the form of an irregular rectangle and did not include a temple of the usual type but a stoa which extended along the southern rampart of the rock. It faced northwards and had two wings projecting from its western and eastern edge (Plan 5). The entire western portion of the Brauronion, which has nowadays vanished, rested on the Mycenaean rampart. Of its eastern section only the cuttings in the rock to receive the walls plus some poros-stone blocks *in situ* have been preserved (Pl. 28a-b, 29a).

In one of the wings was the cult statue of the goddess surely of wood, which showed her seated probably copying the statue at Brauron. Women invoking her aid attired the revered statue with robes. From the year 346 B.C. (IG II^2 1514 - 7 and 1522 - 4) a second statue existed which, according to Pausanias, was a work of the sculptor Praxiteles. It is believed that the type of that statue is rendered

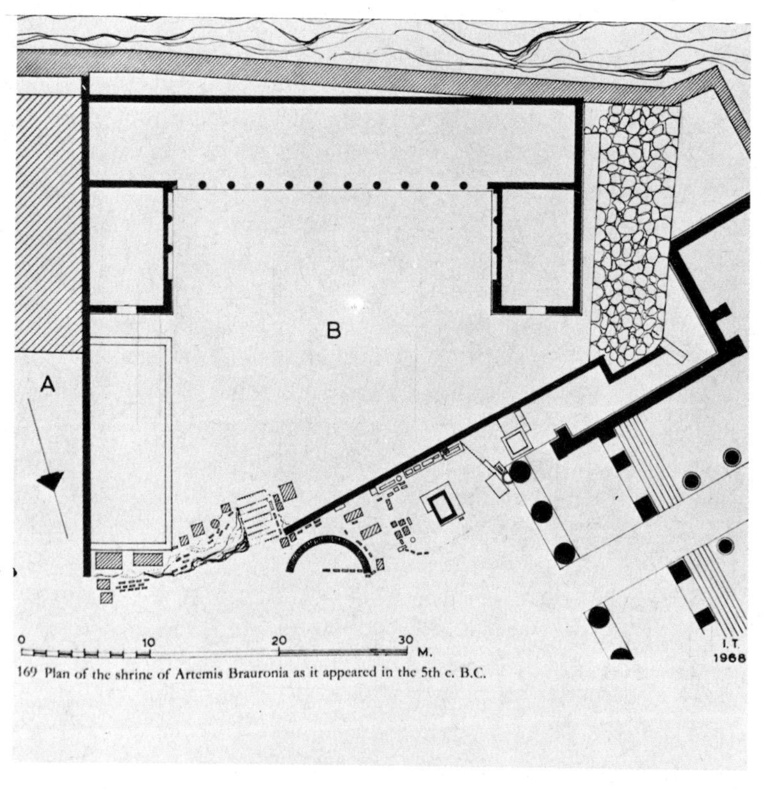

169 Plan of the shrine of Artemis Brauronia as it appeared in the 5th c. B.C.

Plan 5

by the so-called Artemis of Gabii in the Louvre Museum (Lippold, pl. 83, 4. p. 239).

The entrance to the shrine was on the north-east edge of the sanctuary (towards the processional route) where seven steps are hewn out of the rock (see chapter on Athena Hygieia) (Pl. 29b). These steps as well as the northern boundary of the sanctuary which was modelled in the profile of the rock (Pl. 30a) (in ancient times the height was completed with masonry, Pl. 30b, a section of which remains at the west edge of the profile) were made by Mnesicles the architect of the Propylaea.

CHALKOTHEKE (BRONZE STOREROOM)

The foundations to the east of the Brauronion belong to an oblong building which was attached to the southern rampart of the Acropolis (Plan 6). This is believed to be the Chalkotheke mentioned only in inscriptions and intended to house mainly metal votives. The decree (IG II² 120) of the 4th century B.C. ordered the cataloguing of all the objects to be found in the Chalkotheke and the incising of this list on a stone stele to be set up before it :

That the Prytanes order Eukles of the public to come to the Acropolis in order to list the contents of the Chalkotheke... after everything is examined and catalogued, the secretary of the Boule shall write down on a stone stele which will be set up in front of the Chalkotheke.

Also important is the catalogue included in the inscription IG II² 1430 and Hesperia 1938, p. 181 et seq., equally of the 4th century.

Today all that remains of the building are the poros-

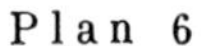
Plan 6

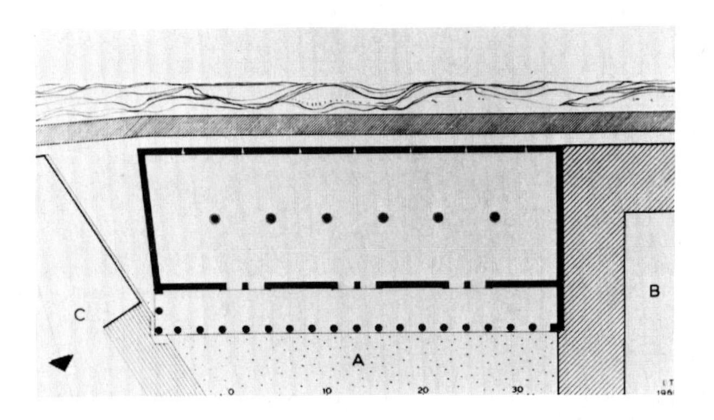

stone blocks from its foundations (Pl. 32 - 33) and cuttings in the rock to receive the foundations at the points where they have vanished. Noteworthy is the north-eastern corner of the building (Pl. 31) because for its foundation a part of the rock-cut steps extending from north to south, west of the Parthenon, had to be destroyed, attesting that it was made after the cutting of the steps. The most likely period for the building is the middle of the 5th century B.C. but the afore-mentioned foundation belongs to a stoa which was added along the length of the north façade of the building at the beginning of the 4th century B.C. In the Roman period it seems that the building was repaired quite extensively (AE 1909, p. 213 et seq.) as various architectural members scattered over the Acropolis and evidently coming from a building of the dimensions of the Chalkotheke indicate.

PARTHENON

In the southern part of the Acropolis where the rock presents an artificial enlargement was raised up in the third quarter of the 5th century B.C. the Parthenon (Pl. 34) the largest of the buildings on the Acropolis, a temple dedicated to Pallas Athena as the Athenians used to call the martial Athena, defender of their city. The ancient Greeks initially named this building simply the Temple and only a part of it, that located behind the cella, was called by them Parthenon (Parthenon—House of the Parthenos (Virgin); the name being another epithet of Athena). From the time of Demosthenes onwards (22, 13, 76) the entire temple was so named. The Parthenon was the first and most important of the buildings which were built in Athens in execution of the historic decision taken by the Athenians in 450 B.C., at Pericles' suggestion, to rebuild the sanctuaries destroyed by the Persians. It seems to have replaced a temple which their fathers had started to build just after the victory at Marathon in the year 490 B.C. but which they had not yet completed when the Persians destroyed it. In size, splendour of decoration and perfection of workmanship, the temple of the Periclean programme was to outshine every precedent in the Attic architecture. It was built though not out of conceit but basically out of gratitude to the goddess who had saved the Athenians from disaster, had helped them afterwards in so many victorious struggles and favoured them liberally with wealth and power. Of course, no one can deny that ostentation for reasons of political imposition was also Pericles' intention but the love of moderation was so deeply rooted in Athens that the blunder of abuse was precluded. Besides, Pericles chose for the design, construction and decoration of the temple the best that Athens disposed of and many artists flocked from other parts of the Hellenic world which all submitted to the demands of Attic art.

He entrusted the building of the temple to two architects: to Iktinos whom we also know as architect of the Temple of Apollo at Phigaleia, and to Kallikrates whom we have already seen as architect of the Temple of Athena Nike on the Acropolis.

Pheidias undertook to design the sculptural decoration *in toto*, being one of the most renowned Athenian sculptors, whose works had already been set up both on the Acropolis itself as well as in other Greek city-states and sanctuaries. Nonetheless, the immense scope of the work compelled the assignment of its execution to many other sculptors, colleagues and pupils of Pheidias, while the great diversity of the entire task necessitated the employment of an army of assistant labourers and craftsmen. An impressive catalogue of all the specialists who participated in the task is given by Plutarch in his Life of Pericles (ch. 12, 13). There were, he says *carpenters, coppersmiths, stone-masons, gilders, softeners of ivory, painters, broiderers, turners* and also *attendants of them and guardians, merchants and sailors and helmsmen by sea, and further, by land waggoners and horse-breeders and charioteers and rope-twiners and linen-makers and leather-workers and road-makers and metal miners* and to further emphasize the organisation required, he adds *and since each particular art, like a general with the army under his separate command kept its own throng of unskilled and untrained labourers in compact array; to be as instrument unto player and as body unto soul in subordinate service, it came to pass that for every age, almost, and every capacity, the city's great abundance was distributed and scattered abroad by such demands.* Through Plutarch's words one can easily feel the strong pulse of enthusiasm which throbbed in the Athenians' veins, The entire city-state had eventually been persuaded, despite the few initial objections, that the work of Pericles embodied, in the last analysis, its own might and superior civilisation. At the apex of the great pyramid stood Pheidias (*everything almost was under his charge* says Plutarch proverbially), even above the architects for as Plutarch explains *he owed his superintendence to his friendship with Pericles.* Of course Pericles' friendship does not suffice to explain his preference for Pheidias. First and foremost Pheidias had catholic artistic knowledge. In his youth he had apparently practised painting, he was also engaged in minor arts and his architectural knowledge was certainly so profound that he was in a position to suggest to the temple architects a design quite different from that typical of a Doric temple. Pheidias' fundamental virtue was his feeling for the magnificent and the divine which the ancient Greeks emphasised and commended and which Pericles, it seems, especially esteemed. So the Parthenon, though not the most typical example of a Doric temple (such as the Temple of Zeus at Olympia) is certainly the most inspired in conception and perfect in execution. An admirable synthesis of all the refinements which Greek architecture had conquered and resplendent in the surprising wealth and modelled strength of its decoration. In comparison with the scope of the enterprise, the time taken for its construction was relatively brief. Plutarch emphasises this too with the perceptive observation that although the work took so little time it was done to be of eternal value *so when the works arose, no less towering in their grandeur than inimitable in the grace of their outlines, since the workmen eagerly strove to surpass themselves in the beauty of their handicraft. And yet the most wonderful thing about them was the speed with which they rose.* He refers to all the buildings constructed then but primarily implies the Parthenon.

Work on the Parthenon began in 447 B.C. and in 438 B.C. on the very day the goddess' birthday was celebrated the official inauguration of the temple was solemnized. Work on the sculpted decoration of the pediment continued until however 432 B.C.

Let us take a closer look at the building. At the height of its stylobate the Parthenon is 69.51 m. long and 30.86 m. wide, or in proportion 9:4. Its overall height up to the apex of the pediments was 13.72 m. which also constitutes a ratio 4:9 with the width of the temple. Almost the entire building was of Pentelic marble excepting its foundations which are of poros-stone (these, as we shall see below, also belonged to its predecessor) and the roof of the main building which was wooden. The main building was surrounded by a colonnade, the «pteron» as the ancient Greeks called it (Pl. 35) (a temple having a single colonnade around the main building is called peripteral). In contrast with the typical examples of the Doric order, the colonnade comprises eight columns on its narrow side, instead of six, and seventeen on its long sides (corner columns are counted twice). The columns are 10.43 m. high and composed of 10-12 drums each having 20 flutings; these served the aesthetic intention of drawing the eye upwards (Pl. 38). The ceiling in the corridor between the pteron and the main building was of marble and its coffers were painted in gaudy hues. The roof of the main building was entirely of marble tiles a significant number of which have been preserved. On the long sides the tiles terminated in antefixes (two exhibited in the Museum), on the narrow sides there was a sima which terminated at the four corners in lion-heads (two are still on the building) (Pl. 43c - 44).

Upon the columns rest the epistyles which bear in their turn the frieze (diazoma) consisting of triglyphs and metopes (Pl. 38). The serious problem which Greek architects faced concerning the placement of the triglyphs and metopes at the edges of the building has, on the Parthenon, found its most eurythmic solution. In a few words the problem was as follows: It is known that the triglyphs went above each column and intercolumniation but if, then, the end triglyph had its normal position it would leave next to it on the corner of the frieze, and thus of the whole building, a gap smaller than one metope which would be unforgivably unaesthetic. Besides, it was an artistic convention to have triglyphs at the edge of the building because their vertical grooves gave the impression that they held the building tightly and maintained it. This means that the terminal metope should be disproportionately larger than the others, a difficulty which was usually overcome by making the final intercolumniations and metopes smaller so that they approached the dimensions of the others. On the Parthenon, however, apart from preserving and indeed emphasising (for aesthetic reasons) the diminution of the end columns, a gradual reduction of the metopes from the centre outwards was adopted (maximum difference in width 0.105 m.) so that each modification occurs almost imperceptibly.

The metopes were the first section of the Parthenon to receive sculpted decoration. Old, conservative artists worked on them alongside younger, more radical ones. Pheidias does not yet seem to have imposed his presonality upon them; indeed Carpenter has recently reached the conclusion that these old metopes originate from the Parthenon which had been begun under Kimon (see chapter on the Older Parthenons). Certainly the metopes had all been made by 440 B.C. Of these those from the south side are best preserved apart from those destroyed in the explosion of 1687. The metopes from all the other sides are badly damaged, perhaps intentionally as it is presumed that they were smashed by Christian fanatics in Medieval times (the metopes on the south side are virtually concealed by the south wall and therefore did not bother the faithful as much). Each metope contained an independent scene with two figures. Dreadful mythological apparitions became decoration. The eastern metopes depict the Gigantomachy, that is the struggle between the gods and the giants who attempted to overthrow the order of Olympus. Unfortunately the representations are much damaged and one can only recognise with difficulty the outlines of the figures which are entwined in outstreched movements. On the west side was probably depicted the Amazonomachy, that is the struggle waged in Prehistoric times by the youths of Athens against the Amazons who had invaded their territory. These metopes are rather better preserved than the east ones. Mounted figures mingle with pedestrian ones, the himatia are billowing, the bodies collapse expiring, a rapid motion passes from one plaque to the next. The Battle against Centaurs (Centauromachy) was shown on the south side and one plaque, the south-western one, is still on the building (Pl. 40), and is in good condition as are several others of these metopes especially the ones removed by Lord Elgin and nowadays displayed in the British Museum. One is exhibited in the Acropolis Museum and two are to be found in its store-room. It seems that the rest were lost in the explosion of Morosini. The story of the Battle against Centaurs is well-known. A fierce struggle raged between the Centaurs and the Lapiths, people of Thessaly, because the former tried to seize the women of the latter from the wedding feast to which they had been invited to honour the nuptials of Peirithoos, king of the Lapiths. Finally, on the north side were depicted scenes from the Trojan War. Eleven metopes are preserved on the building, the others were lost forever after the explosion. Only the north-western one is relatively well-preserved (Pl. 41) and shows a seated female figure and another female figure standing before her.

Rich robes tumble downwards in a torrent of folds enveloping their bodies. Formerly, people believed that here was shown the Annunciation.

The pediments, i.e. the two triangular spaces formed by the raking cornices of the upper part of the building were the third and final section of the temple to receive sculpted decoration (437-432 B.C.). Here also Pheidias chose mythological themes but ones which were clearly Attic. The east pediment above the temple's main entrance depicted the birth of Athena. In the centre, enthroned in majesty, was Zeus and beside him an armed and vivacious Athena just as she had sprung forth from the head of her father; next to them Hephaestos, worker of the miracle. To right and left other divinities followed from close at hand or attended from afar the unprecedented event. A calm motion pervaded the pediment from the centre towards the two edges terminating there where some of the gods, nonchalantly sitting or reclining, were still apparently ignorant of the miracle which had taken place in the middle. Finally right in the corners were, on the left, the four-horse chariot of the Sun (Helios) arising from the Ocean and, on the right that of the Moon (Selene) plunging into the Ocean, symbols of the new era which began with the birth of Athena and of the old world which then disappeared. The west pediment depicted the dispute between Athena and Poseidon for the conquest of Attica. In the centre Athena and Poseidon, in forcible motion, revealed what each could offer the inhabitants of the city in order to win them over. On the left Athena offered the olive tree, on the right Poseidon proffered the sea. Local gods and demi-gods, relatives of the protagonists and judges of the contest followed the scene from here and there. The sculpted decoration on both pediments consisted of approximately fifty statues in the round projected on a deep blue background. Only a small proportion of them have been preserved today. Even by the 17th century, as is revealed in the sketches of contemporary travellers, the central section of the east pediment was already missing, that is the very scene of the birth of Athena, the reconstruction of which is still one of the most difficult archaeological problems. Morosini's explosion completely destroyed or mutilated a large part of the figures on both the pediments. Elgin later collected and shipped to England the best-kept of the remaining figures. These, together with large sections of the frieze and metopes from the south side of the building, constitue the boast of the British Museum (Elgin Marbles). In the Acropolis Museum and its store-rooms there are still several notable and minor pieces. On the actual building, however, only the amorphous remnants of the two further horses' heads from the Selene quadriga in the east pediment are still *in situ*, the two front ones and the reclining figure of Dionysos being casts of the originals in London (Pl. 45). In the west pediment the figures of Kekrops and his daughter (Pl. 44) as well as a reclining female figure, perhaps Kallirhoe are also copies, the originals having been recently transferred to the Museum.

All these are but fragments of the initial grandiose composition and yet they are the most astonishing examples of the finest hour in Greek art. They speak for ingenious artists (Pheidias, Agorakritos, Alkamenes etc.) who felt the marble breathe beneath their chisels, becoming warm firm flesh, garments more true than the real. They speak for a great creator, Pheidias, who insufflated others with his divine breath, whose glance like no-one else's before or after him penetrated the very existence of the gods of Olympus and who strung out with princely grandeur his figures within the triangular confines of the pediments.

The corners and apices of the pediments were embellished with acroteria in the form of acanthus flowers which climbed up in great curves towards the azure Attic sky. Many fragments of these are kept in the store-rooms of the Acropolis Museum (Pl. 42, 43a-b). Four lion-heads (Pl. 43c) adorned the corners of the long sides. Their prime purpose was decorative because the water was freely shed between the antefixes without passing through gutters.

If for the metopes and pediments Pheidias employed subjects from the myths, for the frieze he selected a theme from the every-day life of Athens, the most formal festival of the city, the celebration of the birthday of the goddess which fell on the 28th of the Attic month Hekatombaion (July - August). According to tradition, Theseus king of Athens had inaugurated this celebration in prehistoric times. In the year 566 B.C., however, the Panathenaea took the place of the city's major festivity with the founding of the Great Panathenaea which were celebrated with especial brilliance every four years. Essentially the ceremony consisted of delivering a cloth-of-gold peplos to the goddess. This had been woven throughout the year by girls of aristocratic families, the so-called Arrephori. Adorned with a representation of the Battle against the Giants, this peplos was brought accompanied by the entire population of the city and with especial magnificence, from the Kerameikos to the Acropolis. At the start it was hung on the mast of a wheeled ship, from the Areios Pagos onwards it was carried by hand. On the Acropolis the peplos was handed over to the priests who undertook the dressing of the goddess' statue (in all probability the old statue of the goddess which was in the *Old Temple*). The ceremony was concluded with the sacrifice of the *Hekatombe*, that is of one hundred oxen. It was this procession which Pheidias depicted on the frieze though he did not, of course, work alone on the carving of it. Apart from the designs which were certainly his, his hand can be discerned with relative certainty only on one section of the east frieze, precisely there where Zeus is portrayed with Hera and their messenger Iris next to them. All the other plaques are the work of his pupils, executors, as we have said, of his designs. Most wonderful is the melody of the procession, of the gods, the total of 360 human figures and host of beasts. The procession departs from the south-west corner of the temple in two groups of which the one unfolds on the west and north frieze while the other proceeds along the south side to meet up on the east side, where the gods are awaiting. The plaques from the west frieze as well as some from the south are in their original positions (Pl. 39) on the building (apart from the terminal one towards the north which is in the British Museum). No other section of the frieze is still *in situ* upon the monument. A small part is exhibited in the Acropolis Museum but the greater part is to be found in the British Museum while a plaque from the east frieze is in the Louvre and a fragment of another in Vienna. Many pieces of the frieze have disappeared completely, either during Morosini's destruction or even before.

Despite the accurate rendition of many elements such as the principal stages in the procession, no-one can actually say that the frieze is a realistic depiction of the Panathenaea. On the contrary, its main characteristic is idealisation. For istance, even the most minute evidence of landscape is missing and, although its phases are readily distinguishable the procession is not represented in its entirety at a given moment but as a development which cannot possibly correspond to reality. The idealisation is completed by the appearance of the gods on the east frieze. On the west frieze (on the building) the procession is presumably still at the Kerameikos (Pl. 38). The horsemen, youths from the richest Athenian families, are still preparing; one is adjusting his clothing, another his sandals, a third trying to accomodate himself on the back of his horse, while the figures approaching the north-west corner have already started off. On the north and south friezes the equestrian figures advance undulatingly while, ahead of them, youths accompanying oxen or rams for sacrifice, musicians, elders bearing olive branches, carriers of water jugs all proceed in a dense but calm crowd towards the east frieze. There was its terminus. The chief-priest received the peplos from the Arrephori while the gods of Olympus, in two groups of six, attended as if invisible to mortals, seated and conversing among themselves, the arrival of the procession.

This work deserves our boundless admiration, not only for its life-like rendering of the figures and perfection in even the minutest details, but also for the musical flow which pervades the entire procession from edge to edge, for the silence which envelops each one of the figures, for the mute and solemn hymn which each one, separately and in unison, seems to be singing to the goddess and to the city.

In ground plan the Parthenon was divided into four parts : a) the Pronaos, b) the main temple or cella, (Hekatompedhos Temple), c) the main «Parthenon», d) the opisthodomus.

In front of the pronaos and behind the opisthodomus is a row of six Doric columns of slightly smaller dimensions than those of the pteron. From receptacles on their sides and the particular elaboration of the floor it seems that they were connected to each other and to the pronaos with trellising which reached the top, thus forming closed spaces which could be used as store-rooms.

Passing from the pronaos, through a great portal (10 high × 4.92 m. wide) one entered the cella (29.89 long × 19 m. wide) which kept the name Hekatompedhos from the primordial Parthenon which, as we shall see below, was truly 100 Doric feet long. The cella of the Parthenon was divided by two colonnades into three length-wise sections and by another colonnade behind into a transverse section at the back so that the colonnades formed a long-legged Π. Immediately behind the east wall, at the beginning of the colonnade and the corners of the transverse one, square pillars replaced the columns. It seems that a two-tiered colonnade formed a second floor all around. Pieces of columns from an internal colonnade were first found by Penrose in 1888 though it is nowadays believed that these belong to a subsequent repair. This took place, according to Dinsmoor, in the 2nd century B.C. Stevens thinks that it took place in the 2nd century A.D. while Travlos says that these columns come from a stoa in the lower town of the 2nd century B.C. (the so-called Stoa of the Roman?) which were used in the Parthenon during the reign of the emperor Julian to replace its internal colonnade which had been destroyed in the year 267 A.D. by the Heruli Pl. 46a - b).

At the far end of the long-legged Π stood the cult statue of Parthenos Athena, made of ivory and gold, one of Pheidias' masterpieces. Some stones from its immense base and, in the centre of the poros-stone paving (4.09 × 8.04 m.) on which this rested (Pl. 47a) a hole into which the strong central mast of the huge statue was driven, are the only remains of this once wondrous work. The statue was removed by the Christians in the 5th century A.D. and more than likely transferred to Constantinople. From thence forth all traces of it have vanished. However, from the descriptions of Pausanias and others, as well as from Roman copies which are however all much smaller than the original and of inferior artistic value (the best-known of them is the statuette in the National Museum which was found at Varvakeion) we learn the following details about it The statue was approximately 12 m. high. Its naked parts were of plaques of ivory (that is the face, neck, arms and extremities) while the goddess' robe was of gold leaves of which the total weight was 44 talents, i.e. 1140 kilogrammes. The statue was hollow, the gold and ivory being investments applied in some way to a wooden framework which was entirely supported on a strong central shaft which passed inside the base of the statue and was secured in a hole in the floor. It had been anticipated so that the gold plaques could be removed at any time in order to weigh the amount of metal used. This actually happened, according to tradition, in Pheidias' time (437 B. C.) and it was thanks to this device that he was able to resolve his reputation from calumnies. Luckless was the goddess for the same reason in 295 B.C. when Athens was ruled by the tyrant Lachares, governor of king Kassandros of Macedonia. He removed all the gold from the statue *for provision of money* and, as a comic poet remarked *he denuded Athena though she was disturbing no-one.* Since Pausanias describes the statue in detail the gold must have been replaced at some time, probably as soon as 290 B.C. and perhaps it was recast in the old moulds.

Serene and reverend shone the goddess in the half-light of the deep. The weight of her body was supported by her right foot while she slightly bent the left one and drew it a little towards the back. Her raiment was the austere Doric peplos which was open at the side as was usual for virgins. A wide-pleated overfold came down to her thighs and a belt fastened the robe around her waist as was the style of the period. A broad aegis (goat skin) completely covered her breast in the middle of which was the Gorgon's head.

On her head the goddess wore an unusually decorated Attic helmet. There were embossed griffins on the side pieces and griffins alternating with deer on the frontlet. In the centre was the Sphinx flanked to right and left by Pegasos constituting the triple base of the helmet's crest.

With her left hand the goddess touched the shield which

stood beside her on the base and the spear which rested on her left arm between her body and the shield. The external surface of the latter was embellished with relief representations representing the Battle against the Amazons, perhaps made of gold. Plutarch, in his Life of Pericles (31,4) mentions that Pheidias was accused of having illustrated himself and his friend Pericles as Athenian opponents of the Amazons because *the glory of the works was pressing Pheidias jealously*. Truly, imitations of the shield which have survived show on their lower region two figures with portrait-like faces, in particular a figure of a bald old man who must be Pheidias. The inner face of the shield was decorated with the Battle against the Giants, probably painted rather than embossed. Close by was coiled, with its head towards the upper part of the shield, the sacred snake of Athena and the Acropolis, *the guardian serpent* which was so closely connected with the myth of the Erichthonios. The goddess' right hand was slightly extended and in its palm she held a Nike, a statue about 1.80 m. high and probably of marble, which offered her a wreath.

Even the high soles of the goddess' shoes bore relief decoration in gold: the Battle against the Centaurs. As for the approximately 1 m. high base of the statue, this was of dark marble and also bore a bas-relief frieze of appliqué chryselephantine figures representing the myth of the birth of Pandora, the first woman.

There are serious indications that the statue base was fundamentally repaired at some time, probably following the great conflagration which caused considerable damage to the interior of the temple (see above). Can it be that the statue of the goddess was also destroyed then and subsequently replaced? Is the type of the goddess as shown by the statuettes of Varvakeion and Lenormant in the National Museum, of the Pheidian statue or of the new statue which replaced it? These and other questions preoccupy students of the Parthenon and up till now have found no unanimously acceptable reply.

In front of the statue of Athena there was, in Pausanias' time, a pool of water to hydrate the ivory which suffered from the aridity of the Acropolis. The traveller mentions this pool, not in speaking of the Acropolis but when describing the gold ivory statue of Zeus at Olympia (V, 11, 5) which, conversely, on account of the humidity of Altis required a pool of oil to keep it in good condition. No remnants of the Parthenon pool, which must have been very shallow, have been found but Stevens (Hesperia 1955, pp. 267 - 270) associates with it the polished surfaces displayed on some of the slabs of the Parthenon in this region. On the other hand it is conjectured (p. 276) that the pool did not exist from the beginning but was added later, probably during the repair to the statue and its base after the catastrophic fire which took place, in his opinion, in Roman times.

Under Hadrian the Athenians set up a colossal statue of the emperor near that of Athena in the cella. A host of votives filled the free spaces, primarily the side aisles. Trophies, shields, weapons etc., mainly of the victors at the Athenian games, were hung from the epistyle and columns.

There was no connection of the cella with the western section, i.e. the one principally called «Parthenon». Nowadays however this appartment is not distinguishable from the cella and the temple's interior appears uniform (Pl. 36, 49) but in antiquity it was divided off from the latter by a wall. The traces of hinges preserved on the floor attest the presence of three doors which, from the technical details, seem to be later additions. One could only go into this room (19.19 × 13.37 m.) through the great portal of the opisthodomus. In the middle of it are four square slabs which were used as bases to support the columns holding up the roof. Since we do not know the height of the columns we cannot easily determine the height of the room. According to one hypothesis this was raised in the centre in the manner, for example, of the roofs of the Mycenaean megara though this is somewhat improbable. This space was used for the safe-guarding of precious objects. Here, for instance, was kept the *silver-footed stool* on which Xerxes had sat while following the naval battle of Salamis, the bronze stele which mentioned the quantity of precious materials used to make the statue of Athena and a hoard of weapons, furniture, vessels etc. From the literary sources we are informed that a part of these was sold in the difficult hours of the Peloponnesian War while others were stolen over the years. Many were replaced, however, in the times when Athens was ruled by the prudent politician Lykourgos (338 - 327 B.C.).

Plutarch, in his Life of Demetrios Poliorketes (Besieger), tells us (ch. 23) that the opisthodomus of the Parthenon was ceded to Demetrios (304 B.C. when he appeared as the Liberator of Athens) for lodgings but it is not clear whether he means the opisthodomus of the Parthenon. Most probably he means the main «Parthenon» which was more spacious and which Demetrios turned into a place of orgies.

From the great portal which, like that of the Propylaea, had wooden investments, one passed to the opisthodomus. In the south west corner is preserved to this very day the lower part of the minaret from the Turkish mosque, built on the inside of bricks and on the outside with stone blocks from the Parthenon. From inscribed accounts of the ancient treasurers it is evident that the Athenians deposited the money of the city in what they called the opisthodomus of the Parthenon. The decree of 435/4 expressly commands that the money of Athena be deposited on the right (presumably of the door of the opisthodomus) while that of the other gods be placed on the left. Here then the opisthodomus referred to is that part protected by railings and not the so-called «Parthenon».

No major changes were made to the Parthenon during the later years of antiquity excepting some additions to the east façade. After the Battle of Granikos Alexander dedicated on the epistyle of the temple some of the shields which he had taken as booty following his victory there in 334 B.C. Their positions are evident from the large rectangular holes to be seen at intervals. There are also other holes, smaller and more numerous, between the circular spaces occupied by the shields. These were used to support the bronze lettering of an inscription of a votive decree issued by the Athenians in the year 61 A.D. in order to flatter the emperor Nero.

Perhaps this is the most suitable place to say a word or two about the level area to the west of the Parthenon. It seems that here the Panathenaic procession assembled before continuing its route towards the temple. From this spot one was confronted with the procession as Pheidias and his disciples had chiselled it in stone on the Parthenon frieze. This area is reached by a series of nine rock-cut steps at a distance of 10.50 to 11 m. from the Parthenon and parallel with it along several metres of its length. Some scholars think that poros-stone steps, some of which were found nearby, continued up until the level of the Parthenon. Others maintain that there was a retaining wall for an embankment which no longer exists. The copious cuttings which the steps exhibit make clear that innumerable votives and stelae were set up here.

Opposite, in the south-western corner of the Parthenon, is a wall (thickness of lower part 1.70, of upper part 1.20 m.) of regular poros-stone masonry (Pl. 52) which forms a right-angle. The branches of this wall, known in archaeological terminology as S4, are approximately parallel with the west and south wall of the temple. Presumably its aim was to create a space for constructional works on the temple as well as for the congregation of worshippers. Because the top of the corner of S4 sits on the lower courses of the Kimonian Wall it is maintained that the former, and consequently the stereobate of the Parthenon, are later than Kimon.

Some scholars assume that another wall, S3, nowadays invisible, which lay further eastward and led obliquely from the Kimonian Wall to the Museum belonged to the same works.

The excavations of the embankment to the south of the Parthenon brought to light, amongst other things, the foundations of a long narrow rectangular building (38 × 13 m.) which is divided by a corridor into two rooms. Because its walls are very thin, in part consisting of older architectural members, marble drums etc. that is the building was improvised, and because there were many stone-chips scattered around it, Dörpfeld reached the conclusion that this was the workshop of the Parthenon which was abandoned after the completion of the temple. The remains of the «workshop» have once again been buried.

Any description of the Parthenon would be incomplete if it was not augmented with a survey, all be it brief, of its aesthetic value. As we have said, the Parthenon is not the most representative example of the Doric order. It is, however, surely the most wonderful, masterful creation, the result of the cooperation of inspired artists in the most replete hour of the ancient Hellenic world. For centuries Greek artists had struggled to surmount the technical difficulties with which the construction of temples, of Doric temples in particular, presented them. They never ceased working concomitantly for the elevation of the temple from a simple functional building into a clear aesthetic creation. Thus in time they improved the proportions, relieving the heaviness, they discovered that by altering straight lines to slight curves they gave life, we should say breath, to the building. In the course of the centuries the curves withered somewhat, the architectural members were frozen, the proportions died. The Parthenon, however, stands in the centre, or rather at the summit. Never has an ancient building displayed such perfection of proportion, such sensitive divergences, such a spiritual feeling for life. «Never did undulation create such faultless straight line, never did number and music coalesce with such understanding and love». But let us examine one by one the aesthetic elements, the beauty, the so-called refinements.

First and fore-most is its location on the Acropolis. On coming out of the Propylaea the visitor does not behold the temple «en face» but its entire body the building being turned towards the north-east, displaying all at once its «good proportion, that is the harmonious relationship, the equivalent balancing of breadth to length and height» (Orlandos).

Ancient Greek temples have three longitudinal divisions: the crepidoma, the colonnade and the entablature. With these the temple ensures its serenity, so suited to its natural environment. On the Parthenon the relationship between these divisions is the most harmonious ever achieved in Greek art. It has neither the very heavy entablature and short stout columns beloved by Archaic art, nor the very slender, dry columns and the unimportant entablature which held sway in later years.

The lowest of the longitudinal divisions is the crepidoma, the base on which the temple is elevated. It consists of three steps each of which is 0.55 m. high (the uppermost is called the stylobate for on this *stand the stylos* i.e. column). The German Hoffner and the Englishman Pennethorne first realised in 1837 that the steps of the Parthenon are curves

(Pl. 48). It was quickly recognised that the curves served no functional purpose, as even later some scholars insisted on believing, but were purely aesthetic. The steps swell towards the centre 0.11 m. totally, on the long sides, 0.06 m. on the narrow side forming the so-called hyperbolic curves. In conjunction with the unusual, for a Doric temple, width-wise dimensions, these successive curves (extended also to the entablature) give the impression that the temple has taken a deep breath before coming to rest on the site.

An opposite movement is required to counterbalance the aesthetic intensity thus developed outwards of the building. The architect felt the need to bind the building with inverted forces by slanting its upper structures inwards. Thus the walls and colonnades constituting the second height-wise division of the building slant inwards so that this forms the base of an immense pyramid. The corner columns have, of course, double inclination and each repeats this movement with the so-called «diminution» that is of their tapering which takes place from the bottom upwards. The «diminution» is not, however, uniform but follows a peculiar curve. At approximately 2/5 of their height an opposite movement is apparent. Resembling a swelling it was called «entasis» by the ancient Greeks obviously because it created the impression of the column's ability to bear the weight of the entablature. In Archaic columns the «entasis» was more pronounced, here it has found its perfect equilibrium in relation to the height and thickness of the column; later even this will be obliterated. The «stepping» of the columns is, on the Parthenon, very careful. Apart from the fact that no interval between adjacent columns is exactly the same, so as to avoid the monotony of repetition (the most significant difference being in the intercolumniation with the corner columns which are thicker than the rest), the rhythm of the «stepping» is such as to create for the beholder the pleasant illusion that the columns and intercolumniations succeed one another at the «appropriate moment» (Orlandos) (each space is 2 1/4 times the lower diameter of the column).

Finally, the third height-wise division of the temple is the entablature. And here – it is indeed incredible – in all its horizontal divisions the architect has repeated the curves of the base, as if he had wanted to move the entire temple from end to end in a huge wave.

The afore-mentioned refinements do not of course exhaust the subject and a retrospective glance at the specialist studies will readily increase their number. All these refinements, many of which are not immediately visible, surely aspired at ensuring for the building a life of its own along with a covert harmony which, as Herakleitos said, is *superior to the overt.* A work of very fine and complex calculations, without doubt the one which demonstrates just how advanced was geometric and mathematical science at that time and also how high were the aesthetic demands of the public.

From Pausanias, as always (VIII, 41, 5), we learn that Iktinos, one of the two architects of the Parthenon was also architect of the temple of Apollo at Bassae in Phigaleia which may be regarded as the twin brother of the Parthenon. Nonetheless, something is missing from the temple of Apollo for it to be a Parthenon. What can it be? None other to be sure than the presence of Pheidias to whom the Parthenon certainly owes its majestic simplicity as well as, naturally, the wealth and perfection of its sculptural decoration elaborated wherever possible yet within the context of Hellenic measure. And we cannot speak of decoration in simple terms for this was, at least in those days, completely foreign to Greek temple builders. Nor can we speak of unadulterated and naive portrayal of religious myths associated directly or indirectly with the worshipped divinity, as was usual in earlier times. The Parthenon presents entirely new meanings in its sculptural decoration. First of all the themes of the metopes (Gods against Giants, Greeks against Trojans, Athenians against Amazons, Lapiths against Centaurs) were chosen in order to be an explicit allusion to the still recent victories of the Greeks over the barbarians from the east. For the Greeks of the 5th century B.C. these signified, more generally, the predominance of the world of order and good government over the powers of chaos and hybris. The Amazonomachy is an especial laudation of Athens whose youths had expelled the women of the east, the Amazons, from the foothills of the Acropolis, and the same eulogy was felt by the ancients who beheld the shield of the goddess as well as the Centauromachy on her sandals and the Gigantomachy which was represented a second time on the shield's interior. This same Athenian hymn was heard yet more loudly and resounding in the other decoration of the temple. Thus, on the east pediment with the myth of the goddess' birth, Pheidias showed the birth of the goddess of wisdom which opened up a new era for Athens, the era of its enlightenment, while on the west pediment the two gods who quarreled once of a day for the occupation of the country demonstrate to the whole world what were the forces which consolidated the might of Athens.

Up until the Christian period the Parthenon remained virtually intact as a building. At some moment which is difficult to determine (see above where the internal colonnade of the cella is discussed) its interior and sections of the columns of the pteron suffered damage from an event which is almost as difficult to diagnose. Conflagration? From what cause? Or an earthquake perhaps? Could it be that then the entire central section of the east pediment was lost or maybe this happened later when, in the 5th century A.D., the

Parthenon along with so many idolatrous temples was converted into a church and with the change of the entrance and alteration of the eastern side of the building into an apse, these sculptures were demolished, compulsorily or wantonly. The new church was dedicated to Aghia Sophia (Holy Wisdom) (later, in Middle Byzantine times, to Panaghia (Virgin)). The so-called Parthenon became a narthex and the wall separating it from the cella was partially pulled down and a triple door added. The temple was filled with frescoes some of which have survived (Pl. 50 - 51). When the Crusaders conquered Greece the Parthenon was consecrated to Notre Dame by the Dukes De la Roche, masters of the city. After the capture of Athens by the Turks in 1458 the building seems to have become a mosque.

Throughout all these adventures the building maintained its architectural integrity and a large part of its sculpted decoration up until the 17th century when the first travellers visited Greece and left sketches of what they saw. However, in 1687 when the Acropolis was besieged by the Venetian general Morosini, a shell sent from a canon of his artillery, installed on Philopappos' Hill, fell on the Parthenon, which the Turks had meanwhile transformed into a powder magazine. The building was blown up and part of its sculpted decoration destroyed. Sections of the building and a considerable number of the sculptures were blown off to a larger or smaller radius, some even outside the Acropolis itself (Pl. 37). During his few months sojourn in Athens Morosini attempted to detach some of the still remaining sculptures from the pediment. He failed because he lacked specialized means and only wrought further damage. In the end he confined himself to the removal and conveyance to his native land of fragments only. When the Turks re-entered Athens a few years later they built a small mosque on the ruins of the Parthenon. The lower portion of its minaret is preserved in the south-west corner and is virtually all constructed of stones from the walls of the Parthenon.

At the beginning of the 19th century lord Elgin ambassador of Great Britain at Constantinople, secured the issue of a sultan's decree (Firman) allowing him to detach and remove from the Acropolis and other Greek sites, ancient works of art of his liking. With this permission, which was granted at a time when the Sublime Porte sought, for political reasons, the friendship of England, lord Elgin launched upon a large-scale abduction of works of art and especially of the sculptures of the Parthenon and the Acropolis in general. These were transported to England and later sold to the British Museum. Thus, the greater part of the sculpted decoration of the Parthenon, one of the Karyatides and other antiquities constitute from thence the glory of the British Museum and are known under the title of Elgin Marbles.

When Greece became an independent State the building was first of all freed from the remains of the mosque and cleared from the ruins. Restoration proceeded slowly, some work was done in 1841, other works were carried out from 1896 (Pl. 37) until 1900. The most systematic works took place between 1922 and 1933. Today continuous conservation work is going on : sticking together of crumbling pieces, removing of iron clamps etc.

Despite the destruction which men as much as time have wrought upon this temple, the Parthenon remains an eternal symbol of «collaboration of mind and heart, the supreme fruit of the human struggle! Space triumphed, small and large were obscured: in the narrow magic parallelogram which he had incised man entered easily and the immense relaxed. Time also triumphed, the fleeting moment became eternity».

EARLIER PARTHENONS

The excavations which took place during the last century and the studies which have continued uninterruptedly for decades investigating the Parthenon's history, have revealed that this was nothing more than the last of a series of temples which were built on the very same spot on the Acropolis. Here from very early times, when exactly is not known, Athena had been worshipped as Pallas, i.e. as a martial goddess, protectress of the city. It is, however, difficult to believe that right from the beginning there existed separate cults for the two aspects of the goddess, the pacific and the polemic. Rather she initially combined both. Sometime however, the separation occurred. On the one hand the cult of the peace-loving goddess remained on the site formerly occupied by the Mycenaean palace and where, later, the *Old Temple* was erected; on the other hand the cult of the martial Athena began being practised slightly further south. The successive phases of this cult, though greatly illuminated by the patient studies of specialists, continue in many places to be obscure and to provoke lively discussion among archaeologists. The following points summarise the achievements of scholarship to date and the dissenting opinions:

1) Traces of buildings for the cult of Athena Pallas older than the 6th century B.C. do not exist or at least have not been found.

2) The first building was probably erected on this site in the first quarter of the 6th century B.C. shortly before the tyranny of Peisistratos. With this fore-runner of the Parthenon is nowadays correlated the Hekatompedhon mentioned in Archaic inscriptions, that is the temple which was

100 Doric feet long (32.71 m.). The name was inherited in succession by the temples which replaced it and the cella of the Periclean Parthenon ended up being thus named. The sole indication of the presence of that temple on the site consists of a cutting 37 m. long running parallel with and at a distance of 0.30 - 0.50 m. from the north foundation of the Parthenon (see Buschor, Ath. Mitt. 1922, p. 95 et seq.). From the time Buschor first proposed the existence of one such Archaic Parthenon, since then known as the «Urparthenon» or primordial Parthenon, a lively discussion has opened up amongst archaeologists as to how its upper structure and sculpted decoration might have been. In broad outline, one faction of archaeologists believes that to it belongs the totality of poros-stone and part of the marble architectural and sculpted pieces of large dimensions from the Middle Archaic period which have been preserved and are exhibited in the Acropolis Museum (Galleries I - III) (e.g. Dinsmoor, Travlos, Harrison et al.). Another faction of archaeologists ascribes these poros-stone and part of the marble remains of large dimensions in the majority to the *Old Temple* (see et seq.) which was located a few metres further north (Schuchhardt, Ath. Mitt. 1935/36, p. 1 et seq.), and assign to the primordial Parthenon only the lioness of Gallery I of the Acropolis Museum which is, according to them, older than the other compositions. It is noteworthy nevertheless that the very first Panathenaic amphorae (566 B.C.) show an Athena in warring stance probably echoing the then recent setting up of a statue of the martial type of Athena (see chapter on Athena Nike).

3) At a debatable moment in time, either after the reestablishment of Democracy (507 B.C.) (Dörpfeld, Ath. Mitt. 1892, p. 158 - 189 and 1902, p. 379 - 416; Hill, AJA 1912, p. 535 - 558) or more likely, after the battle of Marathon (490 B.C.) (Dinsmoor, AJA 1934, p. 408 - 448 and 1935,

p. 508 - 509) the primordial Parthenon was razed to the ground with the aim of replacing it with another building (Parthenon II) which would express the spirit of the new state (Democracy) and would simultaneously fulfill the newest aesthetic conceptions. Its large poros-stone foundation which is still preserved (Pl. 53b) was also used as the foundation for the third, Periclean, Parthenon and is one of the earliest examples of the application of the famous curves. The upper structure of this new temple was to be entirely of marble (Dörpfeld and Hill said: in the beginning of poros-stone, marble was decided upon after the Battle of Marathon), but the Persian invasion (480 B.C.) prevented the completion of the building which had proceeded up to the height of three drums and it, like everything else on the Acropolis, was destroyed. After the retreat of the Persians many of its half-worked drums were incorporated in the northern, the so-called Themistoclean, rampart of the Acropolis and are visible from the north part of the city (see chapter on the Fortification Wall of the Acropolis) while others are still preserved upon the rock (Pl. 53a).

The retaining wall (Pl. 6) distinguishable at the bottom of the ditch south-west of the Parthenon, built of polygonal stones laid roughly in the isodomic manner (the small staircase led to the lower level of the then still extant Mycenaean rampart (Pl. 6) and ran parallel with the south foundation of the Parthenon) seems to have belonged to the same building programme as Parthenon II. It maintained the embankments with which the surface of the Acropolis was widened towards the south.

Recently other scholars have conjectured that the building of Parthenon II was not begun before, but after the Persian Wars by Themistocles or Kimon and that it remained half-finished for some reasons. Pericles, who meanwhile had assumed the government of the State, ordered the re-undertaking of the works with alteration of the architectural plans (Kolbe, Jahr. 1936, p. 1 - 64).

Finally, most recently Carpenter (The Architects of the Parthenon) combining and amplifying the two theories, postulates:

a) Commencement of works on the erection of Parthenon II after the Battle of Marathon.

b) Interruption due to the Persian invasion.

c) New resumption of works under Kimon using the pre-Persian foundation.

d) Change of Kimon's architectural designs by Pericles though with use of the architectural members which had already been carved such as columns, epistyles and frieze (diazoma) including the metopes.

TEMPLE OF ROME AND AUGUSTUS

Eighteen m. to the east of the Parthenon, though not entirely on its axis, exists a rather irregular foundation (approximately 10.50 × 13 m.) consisting of rectangular porosstone blocks of different types (Pl. 54). From Kavvadhias onwards it was generally accepted that this was the foundation of a circular temple without cella (monopteros) of Early Roman times of which many architectural members have been found both here and in other parts of the Acropolis and which slowly have been accumulated on this spot. On the circular epistyle, which faces eastwards, is carved the following inscription in large monumental characters (Pl. 55a):

The people (has dedicated) to the goddess Rome and to Augustus Caesar, when general of the hoplites was Pammenes the son of Zenon from Marathon priest of the goddess Rome and Augustus Saviour on the Acropolis, when priestess of Athena Polias Megiste was the daughter of Asklepides from Halaiai, during the archonship of Areios the son of Dorion from Paiania.

The building then was dedicated to Rome and Augustus by the Athenians. It is obvious that the Athenians sought in this way to propitiate the Roman emperor (Octavius is here expressly referred to as Augustus, therefore the date of the building is after 27 B.C., the year he took this title) because during the civil war between Octavius and Antonius they had allied with the latter. It is generally believed that the most probable date for the temple is between 17 and 10 B.C.

The archaeological remains enable us to make an exact reconstruction of the building. Here we are restricted to mentioning its main features: As already stated the temple was circular, Ionic and monopteros. Its diameter was 8.60 m. and it stood on a step and stylobate. Its upper structure was entirely of white marble and its height until the eaves was 7.35 m. There were nine columns all around and its roof was conical. The fact that its columns (Pl. 55b) imitate those of the Erechtheion leads us to believe that the architect of the temple of Rome and Augustus and he who repaired the Erechtheion at the same time following the fire is one and the same.

One must not, however, omit the view expressed a few years ago by the German architect W. Binder (Der Roma-Augustus Monopteros auf der Akropolis in Athen und sein typologischer Ort, 1969) namely that the foundations to the east of the Parthenon do not correspond structurally with the circular building and infact belong to the Medieval period. Relying on Athenian coins of Imperial times which depict the northern rampart of the Acropolis and the Monopteros alongside the Erechtheion, he thinks that the Monopteros was located somewhere to the east of the latter.

SANCTUARY OF ZEUS POLIEUS

Pausanias (I, 24, 4) says that there existed on the Acropolis: a) Two statues of Zeus Polieus of which one must have been Archaic and the other more recent, a work of Leochares, a sculptor of the 4th century B.C. (echoed on bronze Athenian coins of the period of the Archontes); b) An altar around which the Athenians celebrated a very strange ritual (Diipoleia) which consisted basically of the sacrifice of an ox and was attributed to the mythical king Erechtheus. According to other sources there was not one ox but several and these oxen roamed freely around the altar throughout the ritual, something which presupposes some kind of compound so that the animals could not escape into the remaining area of the Acropolis.

Archaeological research has correlated the site of enactment of this ritual with the highest point on the Acropolis (Plan 7) which, as is known, was located to the north-east of the Parthenon. Naturally this spot was most appropriate to the worship of a divinity of summits such as Zeus. According to Stevens, who has carefully examined the cuttings in the rock in order to reconstruct the original form of the sanctuary (Hesperia 1946, p. 12 et seq.), this consisted of: a) An almost rectangular courtyard entered via its south-west corner. b) The shrine proper which was east and slightly further north of the courtyard. The shrine comprised a small temple *in antis* which faced north and of which only the lower part was of stone, all the upper structure being of wood. In the middle of the cella is a repository carved into the rock which received the ash from sacrifices. To the north of the temple cuttings in the rock and a poros-stone block in its original position indicate that there must have

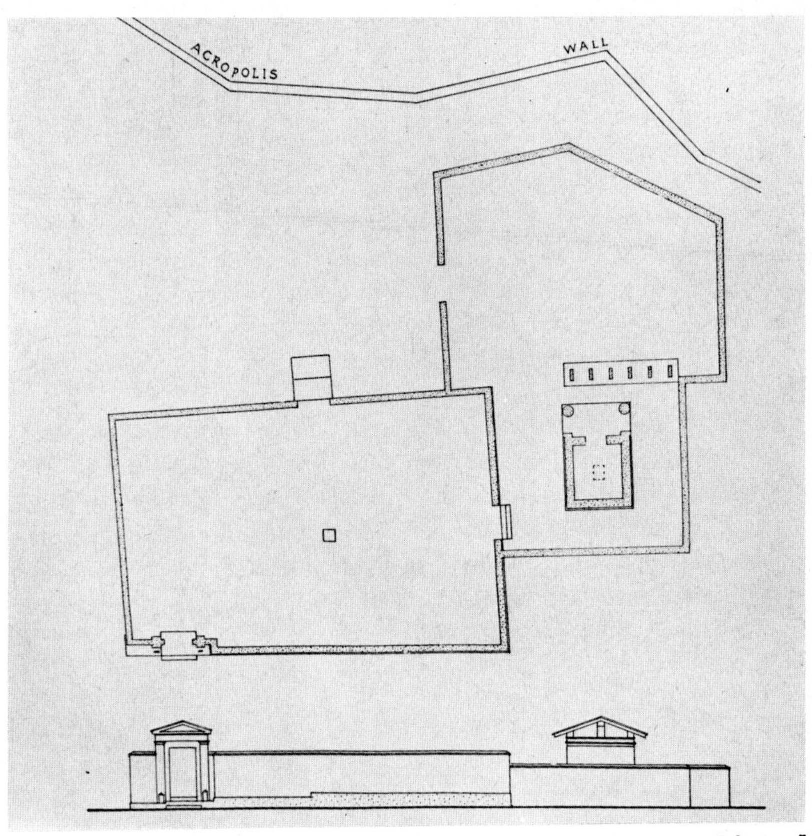

Plan 7

been a long narrow *trapeza* parallel with its façade, near which those participating in the celebration gathered (Pl. 56a).

The rite of Diipoleia is described with minor variations both by Pausanias and the later writer and philosopher Porphyrios. It took place on the 14th of the month Skirophorion (the end of June) and was perhaps aimed at promoting the fruits of the earth. In the beginning, barley mixed with wheat was scattered on the altar and the ox destined for sacrifice was freed. It approached the altar and ate the grain. Then the priest, who was called *Bouphonos* (ox-killer) slaughtered it with an axe and hurriedly disappeared. Since the priest was not seen by the people, for so the rite dictated, they took the axe to court for the slaughter of the ox. The axe was condemned either to be thrown beyond the boundaries of the state or to be cast into the sea.

A strange ritual, incomprehensible even to the Athenians of Classical times, it is nowadays interpreted as a memorial of the transition of the cult from its prehistoric stage, during which offerings of fruits were proffered to the gods, to the more recent stage when blood sacrifices were made unto them.

It is not clear whether the ox (or the oxen) to be sacrificed was housed on the Acropolis during the time of Pericles since information from this period is lacking. Nevertheless, an inscription of 485/4 B.C. prohibits anyone from throwing animal droppings in the area west of the temple, something which clearly indicates that then, at least, oxen were housed on the Acropolis (IG I^2, 3/4).

SANCTUARY OF PANDION

In the year 1887, during Kavvadhias' excavations, the well-designed foundation of a building which he named Workshop was found about 25 m. east of the Parthenon. More recent investigation, however, have shown (Stevens, Hesperia 1946, p. 22 et seq.) that these belong to the enclosure of an important temple (Plan 8). From the ruins of the

Plan 8

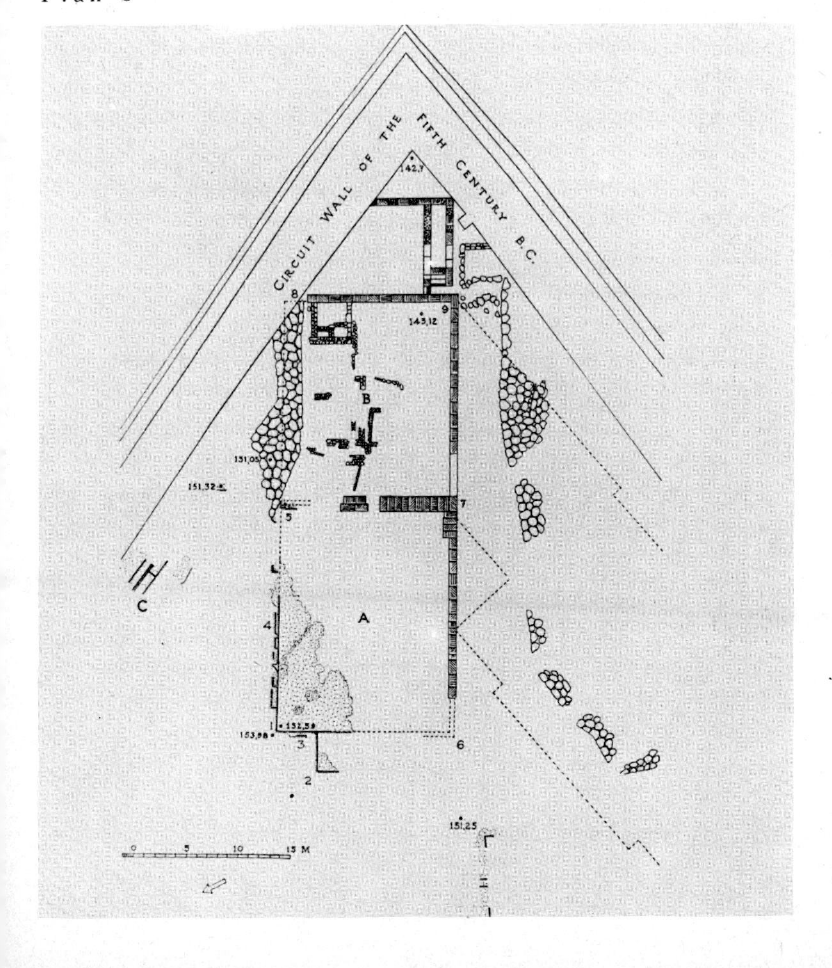

walls, a significant part of which is preserved in the basement of the Museum (Pl. 56b), and the traces on the rock where there are walls no longer, it is clear that the shrine consisted of a rectangular unroofed space which had a general north-west - south-east orientation and was divided into two sections, an eastern and a western. A propylon led to the west space while a gateway existed on the southern wall of the east one. Within the southern section remains of older, poor walls demonstrating the existence of an earlier sanctuary on the same site, were found. When, in the 5th century, the southern rampart of the Acropolis was built, the surface of the south-east corner of the rock was raised considerably and it is likely that the earlier sanctuary was buried then and the new one built.

According to literary tradition the sanctuary belonged to the hero and mythical king of Athens, Pandion. Possibly in this sanctuary the members of the Pandionis tribe, so named after Pandion, performed the rite of Pandia, a festivity basically addressed to Zeus but which seems to have had a political character. Photios tells us that the celebration followed the Dionysia, therefore it occurred in the month Elaphebolion, that is in spring. Precisely because it followed the Dionysia its importance gradually diminished.

One further note: archaeologists formerly placed the Sanctuary of Pandion to the north-east of the Propylaea (see chapter on the north-west area of the Acropolis).

ALTAR OF ATHENA

An altar dedicated to Athena and Erechtheus had existed on the Acropolis ever since Homeric times. The Iliad mentions it (B 550) as altar of Erechtheus *And there the youths of the Athenians as the years roll on in their course seek to win his favour with sacrifices of bulls and rams* but the co-worship of Athena is considered certain. This altar must have been somewhere to the east of the *Old Temple* and would, naturally, have undergone repeated repairs through-out the centuries. Just before the Second World War, researchers attributed to it some cuttings in the rock 15 m. east of the *Old Temple* and almost on its axis. When the Parthenon was built it seems that this altar also served the new temple just as it served the Erechtheion a little later; basically the adored divinity was one despite her several aspects. To one of the numerous repairs which the decoration of the altar must have undergone (we should imagine in Archaic, Classical and post - Classical times) probably belongs the sculpted fragment 2444 in the Acropolis Museum, on display in the hall.

ERECHTHEION

The most elegant and at the same time the most peculiar of the buildings on the Acropolis is the Erechtheion, a relatively small edifice in the Ionic order, situated a few metres to the north of the Parthenon (Pl. 57).

The name Erechtheion means dwelling of Erechtheus, one of the mythical kings of Athens and from earliest times identified with the chthonic demon Erechtheus (if not simply a humanisation of this demon). The building which bears this name was thus called very late on and is only mentioned in Pausanias. More frequently it is referred to simply as Temple, Cella or Sanctuary of Erechtheus in the ancient sources. Its usual title was, however, different; it continued to be called by the name of its predecessor in the same area, the *Old Temple* of Athena and was spoken of as *The Old Temple of Athena Polias* or more plainly as *Temple of Athena* or more circumlocutively as *the Temple in the city in which is the old statue.* One must confess right away that it is not always easy to suggest when these names are referring to the one temple or the other, particularly about the time the Erechtheion was being built when it seems that the *Old Temple* continued to exist contemporaneously for some time. More will be said however of this older temple, of which a first form existed even in Homeric times, in a separate chapter.

Building works on the Erechtheion most probably began in the years of the Peace of Nicias (421 - 415 B.C.) although some scholars maintain that these had already commenced in the time of Pericles and that the Erechtheion is a work of Mnesicles the architect of the Propylaea. The entirely different architectural character of the monument permits us to adopt the view of those who date it to the period of the Peace of Nicias. It is certain that work on the building was interrupted for an interlude. A valuable inscription, found in pieces on the Acropolis, deals with construction activities of the year 409/8 B.C. and reveals that these were restarted in that year with Philokles as architect, otherwise unknown to us. It is clear that the tragic turn of the Sicilian campaign had constituted the reason for the interruption of works (415 - 413 B.C.) and that these were recommenced after the new victories of the Athenian armed forces in 410 B.C.

One of the strangest features of the Erechtheion is its plan which is entirely different from that of other Greek temples (Plan 9). Three basic factors have contributed to it. One is, of course, the unevenness of the ground for the site of the temple is not level; the rock falls away appreciably to north and west and the architect had to find a way accommodating these various levels in one building. The second reason is that the architect was ordered to include within the building as many as possible of the *holy tokens* and older cults with which the temple was associated. Thirdly, the cults practised in the Erechtheion were primarily of a mysterious nature and this imposed a form of building different from that in the case of normal cults.

The Erechtheion was a double temple, basically dedicated to the worship of the two principal gods of Attica, Athena and Poseidon (*gods cohabitant*), the latter having been identified at one time with the chthonic hero and mythical king of Athens Erechtheus. For this reason it is composed of two sections, a larger eastern one and a smaller western one. The internal division, like everything else from the temple's interior, has been lost following its conversion into a church in Medieval times. Nonetheless, the architectural and more general indications favour this supposition as

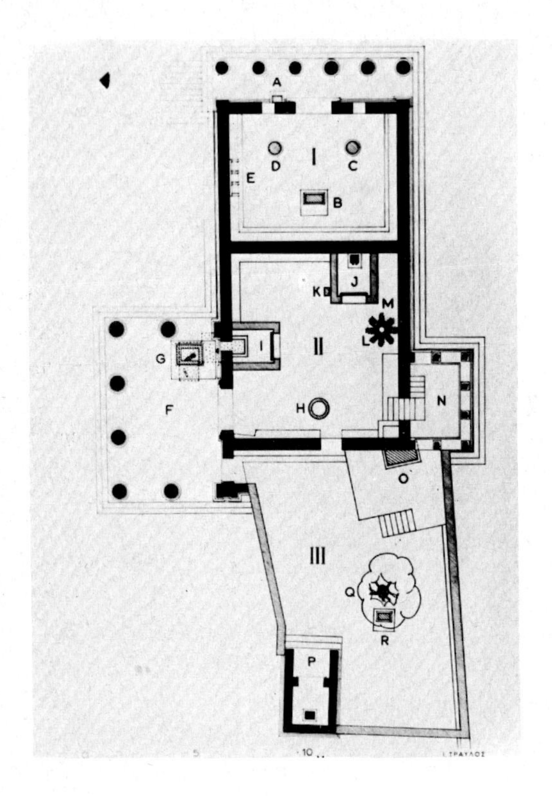

Plan 9

well as the hypothesis that, as in the Parthenon, here also there was no direct communication between the sections.

The entrance to the eastern section was from the east façade and its pronaos was embellished with six elegant Ionic columns (nowadays five *in situ* because the sixth, the northernmost, was acquired by Elgin and taken to the British Museum). It is usually believed that this section was dedicated to Athena Polias, the protectress of the city and that here was to be found her most sacred cult statue in the ancient sources called the holy wooden image (*aghi-*

on bretas), sometimes statue of sitting goddess (*edhos*), sometimes idol (*eidholon*), sometimes wooden statue (*xoanon*) and often simply statue (*aghalma*). Some sources further inform us that this statue was *dhiipetes*, that is that it had fallen from heaven by which it is meant that it was very old. From the lack of description by the authors it is assumed that it had no artistic merit and was probably just a primitive idol. Relevant information concerning its form must be inferred from indirect testimonies which are, once again, the inscriptions mentioning its accessories plus the Attic clay figurines of the Archaic period depicting Athena. Assembling all the elements in a single sentence, one can say that the statue was of olive wood, that it rendered a seated goddess with a band on her head, earrings in her ears, a necklace around her throat, a golden aegis with golden Gorgoneion on her breast, that she held a golden cup, and that somewhere there must also have been a golden owl. The statue received the peplos woven throughout the year by the Arrephori for it is assumed that to it and not to the statue of Pallas in the Parthenon was addressed the feast of the Panathenaea. Once a year, during the feast of Plynteria, the statue's garments were removed and taken to the sea to be discharged of contagion (miasmata) and to liberate, in turn, the city from this.

In front of the statue burnt a golden lamp, a work of the prominent sculptor of the late 5th century B.C. Kallimachos. The wondrous thing about this lamp was that, as was said, it only needed supplying once a year. Above it, so Pausanias says, there was a bronze palm tree as high as the top of the building to *draw off the vapour*. It seems that the ceiling in this part of the temple was wooden and coffered. A building inscription of 409/8 B.C. speaks of the *cross-beams above the statue*. There were various votives here as well such as the cuirass of the Persian Masistios who had led the cavalry at the battle of Plataeae, a Persian *akinakes* (type of short dagger) which was reputed to have belonged to the Persian general Mardonios who was slain in the afore-said battle etc.

In this eastern section, besides the beautiful colonnade of the pronaos of which we spoke earlier, remnants of the cella wall of which the main door was 2.70 m. wide are preserved. From pieces of the door frame which have survived it can be surmised that on both sides of this portal there were two windows of dimensions 2.70 × 0.75 m. Uncertainty prevails concerning the interior of this section because it was totally destroyed in Christian times when the temple was converted into a church (see below). The remains of its internal partition into three aisles belong to this period, in ancient times the space was probably uniform.

The western section of the Erechtheion was 3 m. lower than the eastern one and, according to the predominant theory, was dedicated to the cult of Poseidon-Erechtheus. Hephaestos was also worshipped here along with the hero Boutes, the eponymous hero of the aristocratic lineage of Eteoboutadae. Internally it was also divided into two sections, an easterly cella and a pronaos. The latter had three entrances, one from the north which was the most formal, one from the west and one from the south.

The northern entrance to the pronaos of the western section is still roofed by an impressive propylon (Pl. 58 - 59) (the *prostasis before the portal* of the building inscription of the Erechtheion) which is supported by six tall Ionic columns arranged in the shape of a Π. Although we do not come across curves and fine inclinations like those of the Parthenon in other contemporary buildings of the Doric or Ionic order, in this stoa we discern a slight *tilting* of the columns as well as «entasis» and «diminution» even though these are less perceptible than in the columns of the Parthenon. In compensation, what is deserving of admiration on the Erechtheion is its rich yet refined decoration. Everywhere a wealth of ornamentation yet freshness and lightness (Pl. 60a, 61b). The abacus of the Ionic capital bears in relief an Ionic cymation, the echinus a guilloche and an Ionic cymation, the eyes of the helices (volutes) bore bronze discs, the hypotrachelium (beneath the echinus) a band with relief anthemia, while at the base of the column the upper torus a triple relief guilloche (Pl. 60b).

The ceiling of the propylon (Pl. 61a) which partially originates from a Roman repair, had marble coffers which were once polychrome. With their colouring and metallic decoration they emitted a phantasmagoric brilliance. To the left, where some of the paving stones are missing from the floor, was the altar of Zeus Hypatos on which were offered, not blood sacrifices but libations of dissolved sweets which were poured down an internal orifice reaching the rock at the point where, according to tradition, Poseidon's trident had left its marks (they are visible even today) during his contest with Athena. According to another tradition this is the spot where Zeus' thunderbolt struck and killed Erechtheus and the ancient Athenians sited the tomb of Erechtheus here, this being the reason for the particularly monumental arrangement of the propylon and it was to him that they directed their bloodless sacrifices. The corresponding section of the roof of the propylon was open to indicate the direction of the projectile and because the spot was considered holy it should, in accordance with ancient custom, remain uncovered.

Like the other architectural elements of the propylon the portal leading into the pronaos of the western section of the Erechtheion (the *thyroma* of the building inscription) was also very elaborate. Its initial height was 4.88 m. and its width at the bottom was 2.43 m. (it had an upward tilt of 0.044 m.). A large part of the door frame and its decoration originates from a repair which took place after serious damage, attributed to conflagration, at the close of the 1st century B.C. (Pl. 62). The roof of the propylon was repaired for the first time in 1825.

Underneath the entire floor of the corridor of the pronaos at the western section there existed, during the antiquity, the so-called *Erechtheis Sea* (the cistern as Pausanias calls it), a pool of salt water which had spurted forth from the rock when Poseidon struck it with his trident during his dispute with Athena. Commenting on the presence of sea water so far away from the sea, Pausanias' only explanation is to say that such water also existed in other inland places. He adds that the water of the Erechtheion *is remarkable for the noise of the waves it sends forth when a south wind blows.* Perhaps Pausanias did not want to say that underground springs were closely associated with the worship of a chthonic hero such as Erechtheus.

A small door between the south-west jamb of the propylon and the jamb connecting it to the building facilitated direct communication with the Pandroseion which neighboured the Erechtheion on its west side.

To the east of the north propylon extended a courtyard which was formerly paved with marble slabs upon a porosstone foundation (the only one to have survived). A magnificent staircase extended right along the eastern edge of this courtyard and half of it, that towards the rampart of the Acropolis, has nowadays been restored. Then, as now, the staircase facilitated the transition of the visitor from one level to the other.

In the cella of the western section of the Erechtheion Poseidon-Erechtheus was worshipped with mystic rites and in a mysterious manner (it seems that initially only the autochthonous god Erechtheus was worshipped in this area and that Poseidon was amalgamated with him in Mycenaean times). The hero Boutes and Hephaestos were also worshipped here and there were marble thrones for their priests nowadays to be found a few metres southeast of the Erechtheion. According to Pausanias (there were painted scenes of the lineage of Boutadae on the walls of the cella of the western section. It was here (though some scholars insist that it was in the eastern cella) that the sacred snake of Athena, the *household snake* of the ancient sources, had its nest. According to a view this cella had no roof.

Travlos (Pictorial Dictionary of Ancient Athens, p. 213 et seq.) completely reverses the arrangement of the sections outlined above. He thinks that the altars of Poseidon-Erechtheus, of Boutes and of Hephaestos were in the eastern section and that the wooden statue of Athena Polias was in the western one. He bases his opinion on the ordering of Pausanias' descriptions (I, 26, 5) for he thinks that the chronicler visited the eastern section first, where he mentions the altars etc., and afterwards the western one where he mentions the statue of the goddess. Furthermore, according to Travlos, the magnificent entrance of the north propylon naturally led into the place where Athena was worshipped rather than into where the heroes were worshipped. The three thrones spoken of above were in this eastern section.

A small door in the south-west corner of the pronaos gave access to the pleasant and very famous *Porch of the Karyatides* (Pl. 63 - 65). In Classical times these graceful maidens who seemingly hold up with their heads (through an architectural member resembling a capital) the roof of the porch (the porch has neither a frieze nor a cornice with pediment) were simply called Korai (and the porch the *Porch of the Korai*), the same as the statues of maidens which the Athenians had dedicated to their goddess in Archaic times. The Korai in this instance had a functional, architectural destination a use of theirs known also from earlier times as, for instance, in the Treasuries of the Siphnians and Knidians at Delphi. The name Karyatides came into use during the later years of antiquity. The Roman architect Vitruvius, mentions that the statues of the Erechtheion represented the women of Karyae, a city of Laconia, which had sided with the Medes during the Persian Wars and was severely punished for this by the Greeks who slaughtered its menfolk and enslaved its women. This is but a fictional tale, more probable is that the Korai were identified with the Karyatid virgins who performed, in their home-land, the well-known dances in honour of the Karyatid Artemis.

Without a doubt the porch of the Korai or Karyatides is, and deservedly so, one of the best-known monuments in the world. With their haughty bearing and light tread these six maidens arranged in a Π shape (like the columns of the north porch) upon a podium 1.77 m. high, support the roof of the south porch, looking as if they feel nothing of the weight they bear, and face the visitor rejoicingly (Pl. 64 - 65). Bending one foot (always the one towards the central axis) they bestow a slight undulation upon the entire composition, relieving it of its exaggerated stiffness; their robust, beautiful bodies seem to breathe beneath their garments; simple is their attire, a doric peplos with tuck and fall of pleats after the fashion of the period but without a girdle. Melodious pleats tenderly play between the breasts and fall harmoniously towards the feet. Their long hair, loosely caught behind, frames in soft waves the fresh youthful faces which, alas, time has worn away implacably. The arms are missing from all the Korai but from copies found in the villa of the emperor Hadrian at Tivoli and from another one in the Vatican, it appears that they were simply lowered by the side of the body and that the left one held a corner of the dress. Workmanship, pleating and expression attest strong Parthenonic influences (which is after all natural) and the chisel of exceptional artists. Surely the principal artist, that is he who made as an example (as was the custom then) at least one of these (probably the one at the south-west corner) was a pupil of Pheidias. It is debatable as to who he was, perhaps Alkamenes as was formerly believed (because of the typological similarity the Korai bear to his Prokne which is exhibited in Gallery IX of the Acropolis Museum) or maybe Kallimachos or someone else. The Korai support the epistyle upon their head through the architectural device of a «basket» embellished with Ionic ovolo. The epistyle is composed of three bands (the uppermost bearing rosettes in relief), the cornice consists of dentils, while the ceiling is richly coffered in marble. As already stated, there was no pedimental roof.

In ancient times there was an opening on the west side of the podium through which one could visit the tomb of Kekrops (the so-called Kekropion) which was just beneath the floor of the porch. Scholars nowadays believe that the Porch of the Korai, which has no organic relation to the rest of the Erechtheion, was specifically constructed to mark monumentally the tomb of Kekrops. Immediately west of it extended the shrine of Kekrops which gave the porch such names as *porch near the Kekropion* or *corner near the Kekropion* mentioned in the inscriptions. Careful study conducted beneath the porch has demonstrated that the Tomb of Kekrops, which prior to the building of the Erechtheion bordered the northern wall of the *Old Temple*, was not a stone-built monument but, originally at least, a plain mound of earth in one corner of the Mycenaean palace covering the tomb of some ancient ruler, according to the ancient Greeks Kekrops, mythical founder of the city. A slab underneath the floor of the porch (reinforced nowadays by an iron support) protected the tomb when the architect of the Erechtheion began to build.

Along the entire length of the south wall of the building,

on the so-called epicranitis just below the epistyle, runs a zone of fresh anthemia and lotus buds. Deserving of admiration is the precision of the design, the masterly execution and refreshing breath which emanates from this simple and myriad-chiselled theme (Pl. 63).

A frieze rests upon the epicranitis and embraces the whole building excepting the Porch of the Korai which is separate and lower. The decoration of the Erechtheion frieze did not consist of figures in relief cohesive with their background, but of several separately sculptured figures of white Pentelic marble secured with bindings to a background of plaques of ash-coloured Eleusinian marble. Although many of the figures have been preserved (some are displayed in the Acropolis Museum while others are in its storeroom) the subject of the frieze is not altogether clear. Probably the myths of the old kings of Athens, Kekrops, Erechtheus et al., were portrayed. The figures of the frieze of the north porch are somewhat larger than those of the frieze surrounding the main body of the building (Pl. 66a - b, 67a - b).

The west wall of the Erechtheion is called in the inscriptions *that facing the Pandroseion* because it looked towards the adjacent sanctuary of Pandrosos, one of the daughters of Kekrops. This façade of the Erechtheion is two-storeyed (Pl. 68) consisting of a solid wall 2.75 m. high on its lower part (except the little door leading to the Tomb of Kekrops) on top of which was a kind of stoa consisting of four Ionic columns between the south-west and north-west door jamb united below with parapets and above with railings so that the columns were transformed into half-columns. When the building was repaired in the early Imperial years these openings were reduced to windows which were closed with trellising.

The Erechtheion had three pediments; two on the main building and one of the north porch. As we have said before, the Porch of the Korai did not have one. It seems that the pediments were left plain but there were acroteria at their corners in the form of marble vases like flower pots, fragments of which have been preserved.

The above outline is only a general description of the building and the principal «tokens» of the age-old cults associated with this area of the Acropolis and which the architect incorporated within it.

Surely it is now clear why the Erechtheion was the most holy of all the Athenian sanctuaries. When Pausanias says that *Both the city and the whole of the land are alike sacred to Athena; but the most holy symbol is the image of Athena which is on what is now called the Acropolis* and does not extend his opinion to the whole building it is simply because, as the god-fearing man that he was, he hesitated to speak openly of occult rites such as were conducted by the Athenians in the other section of the temple and confined himself merely to a general description of it.

The Erechtheion was built in an era very different from that of the Parthenon. The latter, with its Doric robustness, its grandiose simplicity yet its infinite concealed refinements, indicates better than anything else the power, economic vigour and intellectual acme of Athens during the time of Pericles. The Erechtheion was designed and started at the instigation of the devout politician Nicias (421 B.C.) in an era when the yearning for the distant but solid past, the belief in indigenous gods and demons, had once again expanded in the Athenians' heart. In this same period a wave of elegance and femininity engulfed the Attic art and this building is the loveliest example of the new style formerly called «fine» and «rich». The harshness of the Peloponnesian War, which was only interrupted by transitory armistices, had not the slightest effect on the new artistic current. On seeing the Erechtheion no-one would suspect during what turbulent times it was born.

When the Peloponnesian War reached its well-known conclusion, so tragic for Athens, the Erechtheion had only been finished for two years. In the year its construction was completed (406/5 B.C.) Xenophon tells us (Hell. I, 6, 1) that the *Old Temple of Athena in Athens was burnt to ashes*. Probably he is referring to the old, venerable neighbouring building which had survived the Persian destruction and had been repaired, and not to the Erechtheion as some scholars think. Similarly, Demosthenes' information (24, 136) about a fire in the «opisthodomus» must refer to the *Old Temple* (see chapter on the Old Temple of Athena) which was carelessly repaired after the fire in 406/5 B.C. just when the Erechtheion was definitively delivered from the presence of the *Old Temple*, which hid at least part of its south façade, we shall perhaps never know.

It is certain, however, that at the end of the 1st century B.C. the Erechtheion itself was badly damaged by fire, mainly in its western section and the north propylon. During the early years of Augustus' reign this damage was repaired. At that time the temple's west façade was modified and the form of the great portal of the north porch altered somewhat. The temple, though, was maintained intact until the close of antiquity. Conversely, it underwent serious changes in Early Christian times when it too, just like the other pagan temples in the city (foremost, of course being the Parthenon) was converted into a church; initially of the Virgin (Panaghia) later dedicated to the Holy Trinity (Aghia Triadha). An apse was attached to the east pronaos and the interior was divided into three aisles, the construction of the internal colonnades causing a general confusion of the foundations, while on the north and south walls windows were opened.

Under Frankish rule the building was used as a palace. During the Turkish occupation it housed the harem of the governor. Two reservoirs were built then, one in the posi-

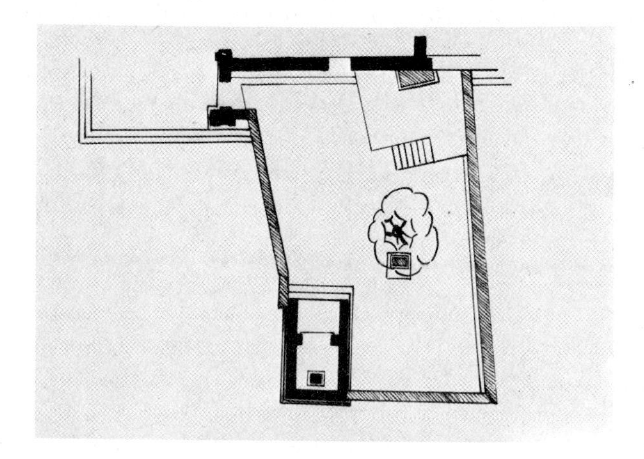

Plan 10

tion of the «cistern» and another in the east part of the north propylon.

During the Greek Revolution, a Turkish shell fell on the Erechtheion (January 1827) causing the collapse of a section of its south wall and of the Porch of the Korai, burying in its ruins the family of Gouras ('Απομνημονεύματα Γ. Μακρυγιάννη, vol. II 'Αρχεῖον Βλαχογιάννη, p. 192). In 1846 the Porch of the Korai was reconstructed by the French architect Paccarde but large sections of the north-east Karyatid which were not found then (some were found a few years ago) were completed by the Italian sculptor Andreoli.

Major reconstruction works took place between 1902 and 1909 (Pl. 69). Work has continued, though on a smaller scale, until the present day.

Adjoining the temple of Athena is the temple of Pandrosos (Pausanias I, 27, 3). West of the Erechtheion was the so-called Pandroseion (Plans 9-10) a sanctuary dedicated to Pandrosos, one of the daughters of Kekrops. West of this site was a small temple which has disappeared as has the altar of *Herkeios Zeus* who had been worshipped on this self-same spot since Mycenaean times, i.e. in the palace courtyard. The sacred tree of Athena which sprouted from the rock when she quarreled with Poseidon has also vanished; it is not unlikely that this tree was originally connected with the cult of Kekrops (Kontoleon). Herodotus mentions (VIII, 54) that the Persians burnt it but it regrew by *as much as one cubit* within a couple of days.

It seems that the sanctuary of Pandrosos existed before the Erechtheion because its position in relation to the latter is oblique and because of the way the steps of the north propylon and the Porch of the Karyatides meet the walls of the sanctuary to north and south respectively. Of the sanctuary some marble floor slabs and two others maintaining the notch of the water conduit have also been preserved.

At the time the Erechtheion was being built, airy and artistic masterpiece of the so-called «rich style» of Greek architecture, there still existed to the south of it a temple of which nowadays, only the foundations are preserved *in situ*. This temple was not mentioned by Pausanias simply because in his time (2nd century A.D.) it had ceased to exist.

Perhaps no other temple has absorbed archaeological scholarship as much as this one. When the foundations south of the Erechtheion were revealed in 1885, Dörpfeld was the first to recognise that they belonged to a large Doric temple which must have been peripteral and amphidistyle in antis in plan (Pl. 70a). Observing, however, that both the material and technique of the foundations is of two different types, he initially believed (with, Wiegand and others) that the building had known two constructional phases. He proposed that the internal foundations of bluish Acropolis limestone belonged to a first phase (about 570 B.C.) during which the temple consisted only of a cella and pronaos, while the external foundations of poros-stone represented the addition of a colonnade (pteron) to the building which took place during the time of the Peisistratids, more precisely between 529 and 520 B.C.

Schuchhardt put forward another point of view. From the number of pieces of the sima (which belongs chronologically to the early decades of the 6th century B.C.), he estimated its length and consequently the length of the temple and reached the conclusion that, right from the beginning, the temple had its large dimensions. He postulated that it was simply modernised by the Peisistratids.

Dinsmoor's theory is completely different. According to him the temple knew only a single building phase in the 6th century B.C. between the years 529 - 520. The architectural and sculptural members assigned to a building phase in the first half of the 6th century B.C. are in reality not derived from this temple but from another one, the older Parthenon (see chapter). Dinsmoor concedes, nonetheless, that a little temple had existed here in Geometric times and though it has not been preserved he considers its existence certain. This must have been the *respected home of Erechtheus* and the *wealthy temple* referred to in Homer. According to Iakovidhes the two bases to the south of the Erechtheion surrounded by railings belong to this temple and not, as was formerly believed, to the Mycenaean palace. These would have been the bases of the wooden columns of the pronaos of the temple of Geometric times (Pl. 70b).

According to Travlos, there were three temples all told on this spot. First the Geometric temple; next a much larger one which replaced it at the close of the 7th or beginning of the 6th century B.C.; finally, a new temple built as a replacement during the times of the Peisistratids.

On going back to the ancient sources in order to find the name of that temple, we recognise without difficulty that it must be the *Old Temple* which is repeatedly mentioned in them. It occupied the site of the Mycenaean palace in the very centre of the Acropolis which was full of age-old cults and religious traditions. The Erechtheion which succeeded it in Classical times has as its cult statue the wooden effigy of the goddess which, in earlier times, was housed in the *Old Temple*.

What has remained of the Geometric temple? Very little :

1) The afore-mentioned two stone bases to the south of the Erechtheion, surrounded by railings.

2) An acroterium of bronze sheet depicting a Gorgon in the middle and surrounded by animals. The significance of this acroterium now displayed in the Gallery of Bronzes in the National Museum, was only recognised a few years ago (E. Touloupa, BCH 1969, p. 862 - 884). All other sections of the temple are either impossible to recognise now or were, it seems, of perishable material which has left no traces.

From the foundations of the 6th century temple one can readily discern its shape and internal division. By the end of the 6th century the temple had a pteron which is estimated to have had six columns on its narrow sides and twelve on its long ones (corner columns are always counted twice). The main building was divided into two sections.

1) An eastern cella of which the roof rested on two internal colonnades. It appears that here was housed the *heaven-fallen idol of olive wood* or *edhos* or *bretas* of the goddess as her cult statue is named in the sources.

2) A western cella which was divided into three rooms. Judging from the subsequent Erechtheion these must have been dedicated to the cults of Poseidon-Erechtheus, Hephaestos and the hero Boutes.

The form of the upper structure of this temple during the 6th century B.C. is, as we have said, one of archaeology's most controversial issues. Scholars such as Schuchhardt who maintain that the temple was built twice during the 6th century attribute to the first architectural stage (about 570 B.C.) the following architectural and sculpted pieces:

1) The poros-stone capitals with very low and swollen echinus (Pl. 53a) and other poros-stone architectural members nowadays collected together by the southern rampart of the Acropolis above the Museum courtyard.

2) The two pediments: a) Two lions lacerating a bull (Museum Gallery III) with Herakles and Triton (on the left side) and Trisomatos (on the right side) (Museum Gallery II);

b) The two lions heraldically positioned (store-room of the Museum) with two huge snakes at the edges (Museum Gallery II).

3) The marble sima with floral decoration (Museum Gallery I-II).

4) The marble Gorgon acroterium (Museum Gallery I).

5) The marble frieze with Panthers (Museum Gallery I).

6) The poros-stone cornice with painted and engraved floral decoration and birds in flight (Museum Gallery I and store-room).

At this stage, as is evident, the upper structure of the temple was of poros-stone and marble combined.

To the second phase (529 - 520 B.C.) are attributed the following:

1) The large poros-stone capitals with a steep echinus curve which one encounters east of the Brauronion (Pl. 71b) and on the north rampart (Pl. 71a).

2) Two marble pediments: a) the eastern one, which is better preserved, depicts the Battle against Giants (Museum Gallery V); b) the western one, of which only fragments have remained, depicted two lions tearing apart a bull (fragments of the bull's head in Museum Gallery I, other pieces in the Museum store-room).

3) Architectural members of poros-stone and metopes of marble which are incorporated within the northern rampart.

4) Marble plaques from the frieze which surrounded the main building (exactly as on the later Parthenon) which was decorated with relief representations of the same subject as on the Parthenon.

5) Marble guttering terminating, at the four corners of the building, in water spouts in the form of animal heads, two of lions and two of rams (lion head in Museum Gallery IV, ram head in the Museum store-room).

Those scholars who maintain that the *Old Temple* knew only one building phase in the 6th century attribute to it only the pieces assigned to the second phase by the others. They attribute all the other members to the older Parthenon.

In 480 B.C. the archaic temple was destroyed by the Persians. After the Athenians re-occupied their city many of its components, as has been said, were incorporated in the northern rampart of the Acropolis. Part of the building, however, probably the west section, seems to have survived, and to have been repaired. This is probably the *megaron* which Herodotus mentions (5, 77) *westward turned* and the *opisthodomus* mentioned in an inscription of 439/8 or 434/3 B.C. (IG I² 91/92). It seems that a marble acroterium depicting a running Nike comes from this repair (Museum Gallery IV, catalogue no. 694). The inscription spoken of reveals that the edifice was used by the Athenians as a treasury deposit of the city, provided of course, that it is referring to this building and not to the Parthenon which was being completed at that time. Certainly the transfer of the Treasury of the anti-Persian League from Delos to Athens in the year 454 B.C. required the existence on the Acropolis of a place suitable to house it. Such a place, prior to the construction of the Parthenon, was none other than the *Old Temple* as it had been repaired after the damage caused by the Persian invasion.

Xenophon mentions (Hell. I, 6, 1) that under the archon Kallias (406/5 B.C.), that is on the eve of the dramatic end of the Peloponnesian War, *the Old Temple of Athena was burnt.* Does he mean this temple or, perhaps, the Erechtheion which had just been completed in order to replace it? The first interpretation is the most likely. From this period onwards, whenever an ancient source mentions the *Old Temple* the dilemma arises as to whether it is the *Old Temple* which is being spoken of or the Erechtheion, for it is still not certain whether the old building was demolished after the conflagration. Demosthenes also speaks of a fire in the opisthodomus (24, 136). Was it then the *Old Temple* again repaired after 406/5 B.C.? After the middle of the 4th century B.C. all traces of this revered and most ancient sanctuary virtually vanished and, in the time of Pausanias (middle of the 2nd century A.D.) the temple, as said at the beginning, had ceased to exist and had been completely obliterated from human memory.

To the north-west of the Erechtheion are the poros-stone ruins of a square (12 m.) building of the 5th century B.C. (Pl. 72a). The main building is a hall (8.50 × 4.50 m.) in front of which was a stoa (4 m. long) open towards the south having two columns between the door jambs. With this building are connected two staircases within the rampart of the Acropolis leading to the outside, one to the cave of Aglauros the other to the cave of Pan (Pl. 72b).

This building has been identified with the *dwelling of the Arrephori* (Bearers of the Sacred Offerings) which Pausanias mentions (I, 27, 3) as being not far from the temple of Athena Polias, that is the Erechtheion. The Arrephori (the word is derived from *arreta pherein* i.e. those who carry what cannot be spoken of) were four little girls, 7 - 11 years old, who were chosen annually by the Athenians to weave the peplos of Athena and to participate in a secret rite which was called Arrephoria. Pausanias and others give us the following information about it. One night during the month of Skirophorion (which corresponds to June-July) two of the girls, holding on their head covered objects, which neither they nor the priestess of Athena who had handed them over knew what they were, descended via a concealed way to a sanctuary of Aphrodite outside the Acropolis. There they left the objects which had been delivered to them and took others, also covered, which they brought to the Acropolis. The scholiast of Lucian reveals to us that these sacred objects were made of dough *imitations of serpents and male members, shoots etc.* from which it becomes clear that the ceremony was aimed at promoting fertility, sowing etc. The hidden descent of the Arrephori is, presumably, the first of the two staircases referred to at the beginning.

NORTH - WEST AREA OF THE ACROPOLIS

Proceeding westwards from the Arrephorion in the direction of the Propylaea, one comes across the ruins of yet another building very close to the latter and attached to the northern rampart of the Acropolis (Pl. 73a). These ruins consist of poros-stone blocks laid isodomically and belonging to a building with two rooms which were aligned towards the northen rampart (the east one is slightly larger than the west one). In front of them was a small stoa of six Doric columns between jambs. The fact that the side walls of the building are bound with the fortification wall is proof that the building was made at the same time, that is immediately following the Persian Wars. In all probability the stoa was abolished during the years when the Propylaea were built and a vertical wall, starting from the westernmost room and terminating at the Propylaea, was put up. According to Stevens, who had studied the matter systematically (Hesperia 1936, p. 511 et seq.), the reasons for this alteration were on the one hand, the wish to remove a colonnade which would have competed with the eastern colonnade of the Propylaea, and on the other hand the wish to create a kind of square courtyard to the left of the exit through the Propylaea, and a corresponding courtyard behind the wall close to their north wing which would serve the sanctuary's auxiliary needs. It is not completely clear what purpose the building served. It used to be identified with the Sanctuary of Pandion. According to Stevens, however, it was probably the residence of priests and priestesses, or even some sort of office.

Before the Persian Wars there was a reservoir on this same spot, the ruins of which are to be seen at a deeper level. It was supplied with rainwater from a carved conduit which passed a few metres east of the Propylaea (Pl. 73b).

THE FORTIFICATION WALL OF THE ACROPOLIS

The Acropolis was a fortress in prehistoric times and as such it required the protection of a rampart. Describing the rock in the middle of the 2nd century A.D., the traveller Pausanias (I, 28, 3) says that *all the rest is said to have been built round it by the Pelasgians, who once lived under the Acropolis. The builders, they say, were Agrolas and Hyperbius*. The fortification wall which Pausanias mentions is the Mycenaean one which was discussed in detail in the chapter on the prehistoric Acropolis.

The Mycenaean rampart seems to have survived until the invasion of the Persians in the years 480 B.C. when it suffered considerable damage by the invaders. As a consequence after the re-occupation of their city, the Athenians, on the recommendation of Themistocles who feared a new attack by the Persians but nonetheless by the Spartans, decided on the refortification of the Acropolis. This took place contemporaneously with the new walling-in of the city, though work on the Acropolis did not take place all at once. It seems that the northern rampart was built first, that which is called Themistoclean after the instigator of the measure. The southern rampart was built later by Kimon, probably following his great victory over the Persians at the river Eurymedon in Asia Minor in 467 B.C. and for this reason bears the name Kimonian (Pl. 74). The Themistoclean Wall is built quite differently from the Kimonian. Many architectural pieces from buildings of the Acropolis which had been destroyed by the Persians were utilised in it (Pl. 75). In the easternmost sector the half-finished marble drums of Parthenon II, which preceded the Periclean Parthenon III, are incorporated in sequence. In the westernmost sector architectural members from the entablature of the *Old Temple*, that is triglyphs and cornices of poros-stone and metopes of marble are incorporated in the same order as they had on the building. A piece of cornice from this series, displaced from its position at an unknown period, was found a few years ago on the northern foothills of the Acropolis in the foundations of the Michaleas mansion which nowadays houses the Kanellopoulos Collection.

The Kimonian Wall is regularly constructed of rectangular poros-stone headers and stretchers to the isodomic system and only in its lower courses are included the epistyles from the *Old Temple.* According to Pausanias, a gilded head of the Gorgon Medusa was attached to the façade of the wall, above the Theatre of Dionysos (I, 21, 4). The Kimonian Wall was built further out than the Mycenaean one and so required the embankment of quite a sizeable area to the south of the meridional brow of the Acropolis. The extension of the Acropolis at this point was necessary to create the space for the construction of Parthenon II, the crepidoma of which, as we have said (see page 84) was also used for Parthenon III. The Kimonian Wall was added to, repaired and remodelled repeatedly in later times. Even in Pericles' day it was raised to the same height as the Periclean Parthenon. In Medieval years it was invested on a large scale with a walling of small irregular stones embedded in mortar. Just after the Second World War the entire south-eastern corner of the rampart, which had showed serious static bending was pulled down and restored.

During the Late Roman period (3rd century A.D.) the west side of the Acropolis received a separate fortification, probably after the catastrophic invasion of the Heruli (267 A.D.). The main elements of this reinforcement, which transformed the Acropolis after so many centuries into a fortress once again, are the Beulé Gate and its flanking bastions (Pl. 76). This fortification was directly connected with the so-called

Valerian Wall, known also as the Late Roman rampart of the lower city, of which many sectors have been preserved.

During Medieval times, apart from the repairs to the Kimonian Wall which have been discussed, the Franks built a very high rectangular bastion on the right wing of the Propylaea (Pl. 77). This was the well-known Koulas which facilitated the reconnaissance of an extensive area round Athens (some scholars believe, i.e. Kambouroglou, that the Koulas was Byzantine). It was, however, impossible to survey towards the east and for this reason a second bastion was built on the north-east side of the Acropolis. The first bastion was demolished in 1875, but the second one still exists and is well-known as the Belvedere.

On the eve of Morosini's assault (1687), the Turks, defenders of the Acropolis, pulled down (p. 52) the Temple of Athena Nike and used its material to build a protective rampart uniting the Nike Bastion with the pedestal of Agrippa, thus fencing off the entrance to the Acropolis (p. 27 - 28). This fortification was part of a great reinforcing enclosure which included apart from the rampart of the Acropolis itself, the rampart of Serpentze on its southern foothills (across the stage of the Odeion of Herodus Atticus), the so-called Wall of Hypapante (Candlemas) on the north-western foothills of the rock. Communication between the Acropolis and the lower city was serviced by nine gates located at various points. One of these was in front of the Nike Bastion and was the oldest entrance to the Medieval Acropolis, dating from the 3rd century A.D. Another one, slightly further down towards the west, on the west Wall of Serpentze, was called *tholikos* because it presented an arched passage. According to an inscription it was constructed in the year 1808 by the voevoda of the city Mustapha ephendi. This Turkish inscription was carved on an architectural member of the Erechtheion and nowadays rests beside its west wall (Pl. 78a).

EX - VOTOS

Apart from the monuments, great and small, there was, in ancient times, a multitude of offerings, great and small, on display on the Acropolis (Pl. 78b - 80). These were very often the works of famous artists. When Pausanias saw and described the Acropolis (middle of the 2nd century A.D.) the Athenian sanctuary may, of course, no longer have been the old hearth of those strong religious and patriotic feelings which erstwhile warmed the hearts of the Athenians; it was, however, certainly one of the most significant open-air museums of Hellenism and for this reason alone attracted visits by lovers of art and of the Athenian past in general. Almost all the votives of Classical and later times have been lost (the votives of the Archaic period survived, mutilated by the Persians, in the deepest deposits and therefore escaped further damage), but many of their bases have remained or even the cuttings in the rock which had received some of them. The principal literary source concerning these votives is Pausanias. In this chapter we shall speak of the major Classical and later votives by combining: a) Pausanias' description, b) the bases and cuttings in the rock, c) the conclusions of archaeological scholarship regarding the types of the works which Pausanias mentions. Guide on our tour will be the American architect, Stevens who has offered valuable specific studies in this field after patient research on the very rock of the Acropolis.

Now as to the statues of the horsemen, I cannot tell for certain whether they are the sons of Xenophon or whether they were made merely to beautify the place (Pausanias I, 22, 4). Today it is believed (see Stevens, Hesperia 1946, p. 82 et seq.) that in 450 B.C. two equestrian statues were placed in front of the repaired Archaic Propylon of the Acropolis. The base of one, of bluish Hymettan marble, is still to be found resting east of the small staircase leading to the Nike Temple. The following inscription is on one of its long sides : *the cavalry men* (have dedicated the statue) *out of the booty taken from the enemy, under their hipparchs Lacedaemonios, Xenophon, Pronapes; Lycios from Eleutherae son of Myron, has made* (it, i.e. the statue). The work, then, was of Lykios, son of Myron.

Pieces from the base of the other group have also been found. Because the bases belong to the middle of the 5th century B.C., Pausanias' proposal that the children of Xenophon were depicted is untenable. Pausanias did not, of course, know how to date the type of lettering and was misled by the name Xenophon. In reality the inscription speaks of three commissioners of whom the first, Lacedaemonios, was the son of the famous general Kimon (IG I^2 40G. Judeich, 229; Stevens, Hesperia 1946, p. 82 et seq.). It is difficult, nonetheless, for us to believe that in the Archaic period bluish Hymettan marble would have been used for the base. It is even more improbable that Mnesicles would have used it in such a conspicuous position. Also noteworthy is the fact that the base does not completely match the underlying pillar of the Propylaea. All these points make us wonder whether the base preserved today is not a copy of the original. From the cavities on the base it is clear that the group was of bronze and that the man was not mounted but was standing alongside the horse (driver of horse), turning towards it, and that he stood fully on his right foot but only on the tip of his left one.

Right at the very entrance to the Acropolis are a Hermes (called Hermes of the Gateway) *and figures of Graces, which tradition says were sculpted by Socrates* (Pausanias I, 22, 8). In the two niches formed to right and left of the entrance of the central section of the Propylaea the floor has receptacles for statue bases. Although this by itself is not sufficient for us to identify these places with the works of art Pausanias mentions there is a strong probability: indeed, one can postulate that the first of the afore-mentioned works was placed in the northern niche and the second in the other. We know that the first was a Hermaic stele and was the work of Pheidias' famous pupil Alkamenes. Its type is fairly well-known from many copies of which the most important are from Pergamon (now in Istanbul), Ephesos and Leningrad, the two former, indeed, bearing epigrams which reveal that their prototype was by Alkamenes.

Copies of the relief of the Graces *(Charites)* have also survived; indeed two are on the Acropolis itself (nowadays to be found in the Museum store-room). They present, however, a serious archaeological problem for the style of the work is clearly older than the period of the philosopher Socrates to whom tradition ascribed it. Therefore, either the type of the relief by Socrates was different or, more probably, the Socrates who made it was a different person and tradition, by the name, attributed it to the more famous Socrates who was a stone-cutter in his youth (Lippold, Gr. Plastik, p. 112). It is more likely that the Socrates of the relief of the Graces was a Boeotian sculptor of the time of Pindar.

The Athenians put a bronze lioness in memory of the woman (Pausanias I, 23, 2). Leaena («lioness») was the mistress of the tyrannicide Aristogeiton. She was tortured by Hippias to betray him but to no avail; for which she was honoured with a statue by the Athenians when the tyranny was abolished. The type of the work is unknown to us.

Statue of Aphrodite, which they say Kallias dedicated and Kalamis made (Pausanias I, 23, 2). Virtually unanimously it is believed (Lippold, p. 110 - 111) that this type of Aphrodite by Kalamis is the *Sosandra* which Lucian praises in his Εἰκόνες (4, 6) and his Ἑταιρικοὶ Διάλογοι (3, 2). It is also believed by many scholars that the type of this work is rendered by a female of the Severe style, which is completely swathed in a heavy, loosely-pleated peplos and is preserved in innumerable Roman copies.

Hard by is a bronze statue of Diitrephes shot through by arrows (Pausanias I, 23, 3). Diitrephes was an Athenian general of the time of the Peloponnesian War who was slain by enemy arrows. The type of the work, which is referred to by Pliny as having been executed by the famous sculptor Kresilas, has not yet been identified among the copies of the Roman period (Lippold, p. 172, pl. 62, 2).

Stevens believes that the lioness (Leaena), the Aphrodite of Kalamis and the Diitrephes were in the following cuttings of the Propylaea: respectively, the statue of the lioness in the cut near the north wall of the eastern section of the Propylaea, that of Aphrodite slightly further east, behind the second column from the north of the same section of the building, finally, of Diitrephes behind the second column from the south, also in the eastern section.

Stevens noticed yet another circular cutting adjoining the south wall of the eastern section of the Propylaea and thinks that here was probably placed a commemorative column which bore a bronze cockerel.

Near the statue of Diitrephes ... I do not wish to write of the less distinguished ... are figures of gods: of Hygieia (Health) ... and of Athena, also surnamed Hygieia (Health) (Pausanias I, 23, 4). On coming out of the Propylaea into the area of the Acropolis one comes across, on the right, a round base adjoining the south corner column of the Propylaea. In accordance with the inscription in front *The Athenians* (have dedicated the statue) *to Athenaea Hygieia; Pyrrhos made* (it) *the Athenian.* The statue portrayed Athena Hygieia and was the work of the Athenian sculptor Pyrrhos.

From the cavities preserved on the upper surface to receive the feet, it is clear that the statue was of bronze. Its type is nowadays thought to be rendered by the so-called Athena Hope (Lippold pl. 66,4 and p. 190).

Plutarch (Life of Pericles 13) mentions that the statue was set up when the Propylaea were being built after an accident which befell a worker. More probably, however, the statue was erected after the years of the terrible pestilence (429-427 B.C.) and as a consequence of this. It has been confirmed that the cult of Athena Hygieia went back to the end of the 6th century B.C. at least. It is also believed that this was not the cult statue initially, but another one which must have stood near the great altar (dimensions 1.45 ×2.20 m.) of which the remains are still to be found *in situ* at a distance of 4-4.50 m. east of Pyrrhos' base. Later however, exactly when we do not know, Pyrrhos' statue of Athena itself became the cult statue and in front of it was placed an offering table whose base has been found (dimensions 1 × 1.70 m.). On the southern side of the south-east corner column of the Propylaea is a large square base, what kind of votive it bore is, however, unknown.

From Classical times onwards, the approach to the Parthenon and other monuments of the Acropolis was facilitated by a road which started off from the Propylaea and proceeded in an easterly direction, dividing the sanctuary into two almost equal sectors (in Archaic times an analogous pathway existed directed further towards the north-east in the direction of the *Old Temple*). This was the route followed by all processions ascending the Acropolis including, of course, Panathenaic procession. A multitude of every kind of votive offerings lined this route and accompanied the pious in their steps. Nowadays, as we have said, only the receptacles of the votives have been preserved and these, not indeed, everywhere but only where the rock was at the surface at that time. Wherever the votives stood on infill they have disappeared without trace. The starting point of the procession route and the cuttings for votives are still discernible on the rock which here corresponds to the ancient surface. So the processional way is certified through the testimony of the transverse notches that facilitated the ascent of the faithful. At one point, near the Propylaea, the road is intersected by quite a wide, deep conduit orientated in a north-easterly direction which collected rain-water and channelled it into reservoir located east of the north wing of the Propylaea (p. 45).

Directly to the right of the south wall of the Propylaea the rock, which is here preserved at a much higher level (Brauronion), is cut vertically towards the procession route for several metres eastwards; then it is interrupted by seven steps hewn out of the rock which led to the Sanctuary of the Brauronian Artemis.

There is the horse called Wooden set up in bronze (Pausanias I, 23, 8). Large rectangular sections of an enormous marble base which bore a larger-than-life statue of the wooden Horse were found during excavations. According to the preserved inscription (IG I² 535), the work was dedicated by one Chairedemos from the demos of Koile and its sculptor was Strongylion. *Chairedemos, the son of Evangelos from the demos of Koile has dedicated* (the statue); *Strongylion has made* (it). The work was set up in about 415 B.C. (Lippold, p. 189).

Just before mentioning the Sanctuary of Artemis, Pausanias speaks of the statue of Perseus (I, 23, 8) who had cut off the head of Medusa, a work of Myron; and a statue of a boy holding a sprinkler, a work of Lykios, son of Myron.

After the Wooden Horse, Pausanias mentions the statue of an infantry-man (hoplite) Epicharinos (I, 23, 9), a work of Kritios. A bronze copy of this is believed to be the one in Tübingen (Lippold, pl. 34, 2 and p. 107).

In this place is a statue of Athena striking Marsyas the Silenus- - -. Opposite these- - - is represented the fight which legend says Theseus fought with the so-called Bull of Minos (Pausanias I, 24, 1). Pausanias, without mentioning that he was in front of the courtyard formed on the west side of the Parthenon, describes two more sculpted votives :

a) Athena and Marsyas, a work of Myron, which is known mainly from copies of Athena in Frankfurt and of Marsyas in the Lateran Museum (Lippold, pl. 49, 3 and 4, p. 139), and b) the struggle of Theseus with the Minotaur, also a work of Myron, which is partially known from copies such as the torse of Minotaur from the Tower of the Winds which is in the National Museum. On examining the rock in this area it has been confirmed that two of the cuttings fit in well with these groups.

Further on, Pausanias (I, 24, 2 et seq.) refers to a statue of Phrixos sacrificing a ram, of Herakles drowning the snakes, of Athena springing forth from the head of Zeus and of a bull offering of the High Court (Areopagos). Of all these votives it has not been possible to identify the position of even one.

In and amongst these offerings, Pausanias also mentions, very vaguely, Athena Ergane. It is not easy to say whether he is referring to a sanctuary of the goddess, a statue of her or to some votive or other. Stevens, however, believes that it concerns a sanctuary, a view which he bases on five inscriptions dedicated to Athena Ergane. Two of these were found in the north-west corner of the Parthenon. On carefully inspecting the area, Stevens observed that (Pl. 78b) a row of shallow cuts, suitable for a monument of considerable size, exists there. Since there are other cuttings nearby, Stevens thought that the monument pre-existed the Persian destruction and was re-built after the expulsion of the Persians on the site mentioned by Pausanias.

- - - *and an image of Earth beseeching Zeus to rain upon her* (Pausanias I, 24, 3). The exact position of this statue is known because, at a distance of 26.50 m. from the north-west corner of the Parthenon and 8.50 m. to the north, the following inscription is carved upon the rock protected by a railing. *Of the fructiferous Gaia according to the oracle.* Adjoining it is a smooth rectangular surface (Pl. 79) where a statue of Gaia (Earth) was set up, probably only from the waist upwards, as if emerging from the rock, her hands extended in supplication towards the sky as she is depicted on vases (Stevens, Hesperia 1946, p. 4, pl. 1). The work was evidently offered during some period of drought and, judging from the characters of the inscription, this must have been during the 2nd century A.D. A little further on exists a series of reservoirs carved into the rock and destined to collect rain-water. It seems that these also belong to the Roman period.

There also are set up Timotheus the son of Konon and Konon himself (Pausanias I, 24, 3). 2.70 m. east of the statue of Gaia is a section of a semi-circular marble base bearing, on its front face, the inscription *Konon of Timotheus, Timotheus of Konon* which evidently supported the statues mentioned by Pausanias. Initially the pedestal was not set up here but some 5.50 m. to the east of the statue of Gaia where a corresponding cutting is preserved. The pedestal is composed of four sections but from the position of the lettering (the name Konon is in the centre, the name of his son Timotheus is squeezed to the right of it), Stevens drew the conclusion that originally (at the beginning of the 4th century), only Konon's statue had been erected on the pedestal along with the trophies of his victory against the Spartan fleet outside Knidos in 394 B.C. and that only after the death of his son, around the middle of the 4th century B.C., was his statue also added, slightly displacing that of his father.

The semi-circular shape of the pedestal considerably aided the presentation of the work which the visitor spotted from afar and followed during his passage next to the monument.

Prokne too, who has already made up her mind about the boy, and Itys as well, a group dedicated by Alkamenes (Pausanias I, 24, 3). The statue of Prokne was discovered in the excavations and nowadays dominates the last Gallery of the Acropolis Museum. According to Stevens, its original position was to the north-east of the Parthenon (at a distance of 3.2 m.) where there is a rectangular cutting in the rock.

Athena is represented displaying the olive plant and Poseidon the wave (Pausanias I, 24, 3). This composition is depicted on Athenian coins of the Imperial period. Poseidon, with one foot on the rock and a trident in his right hand, was conversing amicably with Athena who rested her left hand on her shield. Stevens believed that this work was placed on a rectangular cutting just before the north-east corner of the Parthenon and 2.50 m. east of the statue of Prokne.

There is an approximately square cut (4.43 × 4.90 m.) on the north-east side of the Parthenon. Pausanias does not say anything about the statue it should have received but Stevens located on it a base uncovered by N. Balanos here. It is incomplete and bears the following inscription on one of its sides, in characters of the middle of the 5th century B.C... *the son of Pronapides Pronapes victor at the Nemea, the Isthmia, the Panathenaea* (nowadays resting by the south wall in the Parthenon).

- - - *and there are statues of Zeus, one made by Leochares and one called Polieus* (Protector of the city) (Pausanias I, 24, 4). The statues mentioned by Pausanias evidently stood in the Sanctuary of Zeus Polieus, the position of which was identified, as has been said (p. 89) by Stevens, on the highest point of the rock north-east of the Parthenon. The types of the statues are rendered on bronze Athenian coins. One statue showed Zeus in an aggressive stance with wide stride, left hand outstretched and the right one raised to hurl a thunderbolt. The other showed the god in a calm attitude with his left hand slightly extended. The first type seems to be Late Archaic, the second Early Classical.

- - - *and at the entrance* (to the Parthenon) *one* (statue) *of Iphikrates who accomplished many remarkable achievements* (Pausanias I, 24, 7). Iphikrates was an Athenian general of the 4th century B.C. who served as leader of the mercenaries. The type of the statue has not yet been recognised.

Opposite the temple is a bronze Apollo, said to be the work of Pheidias. They call it the Parnopios (Locust God) because once when locusts were devastating the land the god said he would drive them from Attica (Pausanias I, 24, 8). Pausanias' topographical indication is not clear and we know neither how far from the Parthenon nor in which particular direction the Parnopios Apollo of Pheidias was located. Its type, however, has been known for many years from its several copies which, from the home of the best one, is customarily called the Apollo of Kassel (E. M. Schmidt, Der Kasseler Apollo und seine Repliken, Antike Plastik V).

At this point in his wanderings Pausanias mentions the statues of Pericles and his father Xanthippos (I, 25, 1), adding that *Pericles stands apart* and speaks of his statue again when leaving the Acropolis apparently because it was to be found there. The statue of Xanthippos, however, whose type is still in dispute, was evidently to be found here.

Conversely, the type of the statue of the poet Anakreon is known. According to Pausanias it *stands near Xanthippos* and *his posture is as it were that of a man singing when he is drunk*. The iconographic type is verified from an inscribed bust in the Conservatori Museum in Rome. The best copy is in Copenhagen because, apart from its other virtues, it renders the entire statue and seems to substantiate the suggestion that the artist was either Pheidias himself or one of his immediate collaborators.

By the south wall are represented the legendary War with the giants, who once dwelt about Thrace and on the isthmus of Pallene, the battle between the Athenians and the Amazons, the engagement with the Persians at Marathon and the destruction of the Gauls at Mysia, all were dedicated by Attalos. Emerging from the east entrance of the Parthenon, Pausanias saw four votive sculptural groups on the southern rampart (I, 25, 2). These had been consecrated on the Acropolis by Attalos I, king of Pergamon and their subjects were: a) Battle against the Giants, b) Battle against the Amazons, c) The Battle of Marathon, d) The destruction of the Gauls in Mysia in Asia Minor by the Pergamenes. The statues were, according to Pausanias, *each about two cubits high* and it is as a consequence of their diminutive size and conspicuous position that Dionysos of the Gigantomachy fell down into the Theatre of Dionysos during the course of a violent storm shortly before the naval battle of Actium. From the host of works of the Attalic votive offering only ten are known to us, and these only from copies kept in various museums.

Where the statues of Olympiodoros, an Athenian general who liberated the city from the Macedonians in 286 B.C., and of Artemis Leukophryene stood we cannot tell (Pausanias I, 26, 4).

--- *a statue of Athena seated, with an inscription that Kallias dedicated the image, but Endoios made it* (Pausanias I, 26, 4). We are now conveyed towards the Erechtheion. With this work is identified an Archaic statue of a seated Athena which is exhibited in the Acropolis Museum (Gallery IV, catalogue no. 625). The statue was discovered cast down on the northern slope of the Acropolis below the Erechtheion, that is exactly beneath the spot where Pausanias saw the Athena of Endoios. Endoios was a very well-known artist of pre-Persian Archaic times and the fact that the statue exhibits marked erosion from weather conditions means that it escaped destruction by the Persians. This leads us to believe that it is the very Athena of Endoios which Pausanias saw as he advanced towards the Erechtheion (Lippold, p. 74).

By the temple of Athena - - - an old woman Eueris [?] (or *Syeris*) *about a cubit high, the inscription calling her the handmaid of Lysimache* (Pausanias I, 27, 4). This passage of Pausanias follows his description of the Erechtheion and of the Pandroseion and is one of his most obscure for neither the writing is unanimously accepted nor is its content clear. Does Pausanias speak of one person or two? Does he speak of a Lysimache or of a Syeris? In the Acropolis excavations two statue bases were found; one, according to its inscription, bore a statue of Lysimache who, as Pliny tells us (Naturalis Historia 34, 76), was priestess of Athena for 64 years. The work was by the sculptor Demetrios of Alopeke, famous for his realism. The other base bore a much smaller statue, concordant with its inscription, that of one deaconess Syeris. This was a work of one Nikomachos, sculptor of the 4th century B.C. Does Pausanias mention her only? An iconographic type of an old woman which could be Lysimache has been recognised thanks to a torso in the Basle Museum and a head in the British Museum (Berger, Antike Kunst 1968, p. 67 - 70, pl. 31 - 33) but the whole issue is still far from its definitive solution.

- - - a bronze Athena, tithe from the Persians who landed at Marathon (Pausanias I, 28, 2). The most significant of the works mentioned by Pausanias in the area between the Erechtheion and the Propylaea was a colossal bronze statue of the Promachos Athena, a work of Pheidias. It was situated

in about the middle of that area, slightly to the left of the procession route (for whoever looks eastwards). Several stone blocks from its base have been preserved *in situ* while the whole of its base has been verified from cuttings in the rock. Though Pausanias connects the statue with the Athenian victory at Marathon, Demosthenes (19, 272) simply says that the city had donated the great Athena as *meed of valour of the war against the Persians* and that *the funds were given by the Greeks.* Two American scholars, Dinsmoor and Meritt, having studied an inscription referring to the handling of the money spent on setting up the statue, reached the conclusion that the decision to erect it was taken straight after the triumphant victory of the Athenians over the Persians at the river Eurymedon in Asia Minor in the year 465 B.C. This date also fits the period of the work as we know it from some small-scale imitations. The work was one of Pheidias' earliest. The goddess stood tranquilly wearing a long doric peplos, belted around the waist, and a Corinthian helmet on her head. Her left hand, held down, rested on the shield which was embellished with the Battle against Centaurs in relief, executed by the famous bronze-turner Mys in accordance with designs made for him by Parrhasios, son of Euenor. Her left arm rested upon her spear while in her right hand she held an owl. According to an ancient tradition, mentioned by Pausanias, the tip of her spear and the crest of her helmet were visible to those approaching the shore from the direction of Sounion. The base of the statue was analogous in size with the work, wide but relatively low, so that the pilgrims could admire the Centauromachy on the shield. Until a few years ago it was believed that the upper part of the base was decorated with a large band of enormous eggs and astragals beneath, of which a piece was found in the vicinity of the statue's site (visible to the visitor who crosses the Propylaea) and other fragments in the Museum store-room and elsewhere (Dinsmoor, Χαριστήριον 'Ορλάνδου, p. 144, 145) (Pl. 80). Today, however, this ornamentation is assigned to a repair to the pedestal which took place in Roman times. The statue remained *in situ* until the period of Justinian when it was conveyed to Constantinople. In 1203, on the eve of the sacking of the city by the Franks, it was destroyed by the frenzied mob who thought that with her right hand (from which, meanwhile, the owl had been lost) the goddess beckoned the invaders.

Then there is a bronze chariot, tithe from the Boeotians and the Chalkidians in Euboea (Pausanias I, 28, 2). The trophy was set up following the victory of the Athenians in 507 B.C. against the Boeotians. On that day the Athenians captured many Chalkidian prisoners of war; the chains with which they shackled them were dedicated to the Acropolis and of the tithe of the booty they made a chariot (one of the horses of this chariot thought by some scholars to be that in the courtyard of the Museum) which Herodotus saw to the left of the Propylaea, evidently the building which preceded the Mnesiclean Propylaea. The work also bore an inscription telling of the chains with which the Athenians bound their enemies. Today, two damaged bases are preserved bearing virtually identical inscriptions. One of these belongs to the 6th century B.C. while the other is of the middle of the 5th century. From this we conclude that: a) the original chariot was destroyed or removed by the Persians in 480 B.C., b) the Athenians set up another one immediately after 450 B.C. when they once again vanquished the Chalkidians. This second votive is the one which Herodotus saw outside the pre-Mnesiclean Propylon and Pausanias saw near the Promachos, where to it was evidently moved when the Propylaea of Mnesicles were constructed. The exact position of the new base was, according to Stevens, near the west wall of the old temple of Athena. On examining the area around the Promachos, Stevens verified the existence of numerous other rather shallow cuttings (depth 0.50 m.) which could have supported other trophies set up here in a suitable position facing the visitor who had just crossed the Propylaea.

Shortly before quitting the Acropolis, Pausanias mentions two further statues (I, 28, 2) : one of Lemnia Athena and one of Pericles. The former is known principally from the replica of the torso which is in Dresden and the copy of the head which is in Bologna; of the second, the type of the head is known from Hermaic copies in the British Museum and the Vatican. Unfortunately, Pausanias' description concerning the location of the works is incomplete and, as is usual, one can only guess this. Stevens maintains that a cutting to the north-east of the Propylaea between the first and second columns to the north, fits as the position of the statue of Lemnia. Since Pausanias mentions Lemnia and Pericles together, the latter would have been somewhere very near (according to Stevens), for instance on the same line but further east.

SANCTUARY OF PANDEMOS APHRODITE

Just before coming out of the Beulé Gate one notices to the south, i.e. on the left, the sections of an epistyle decorated with garlands and doves (Pl. 81). In agreement with the inscription which this epistyle bears (IG II² 1531b *this temple, oh'mighty Aphrodite...*) this derives from a little temple dedicated to Aphrodite. The sanctuary of Pandemos Aphrodite is referred to by Pausanias (I,22,3) and from the sequence of his description it is inferred that it was situated somewhere near the Nike Bastion. Up until 1960 research placed it in the western part of the Acropolis. In that year a minor excavation conducted by the Ephorate of the Acropolis (ΠΑΕ 1960, p. 4 - 9) in the shallow area behind the Odeion of Herodes Atticus brought to light finds coming, certainly, from a Sanctuary of Aphrodite (sherds with votive inscriptions, fragments of figurines representing Aphrodite and Eros etc.). Thus it became clear that the shrine was in the south-west part of the Acropolis, precisely on a level rocky area directly beneath the Nike Bastion. In this area the monument of the hero Aegeus was formerly supposed to have been and the rock surface displays superficial incisions testifying the existence of a small temple of the dimensions of the afore-mentioned epistyle. The hypothesis that this was the site of the Temple of Pandemos Aphrodite is strengthened by the observation that next to this site, on the rock front of the Nike Bastion, several shallow niches have been carved for the reception of votives, identical with those existing in other shrines of Aphrodite such as the one on the northern slope of the Acropolis, Daphni etc. (L. Beschi, Annuario XLV - XLVI (1967 - 1968), p. 517 et seq.).

PLATES

General view of the Acropolis from the Pnyx (west).

PLATE 2

Architectural members from churches of Byzantine times (old photograph).

Turkish settlement beside the monuments of the Acropolis (old engraving).

a. Column base and steps of the Mycenaean palace.
b. Section of the Cyclopean (Mycenaean) rampart, east of the Museum.

Section of the Cyclopean (Mycenaean) rampart to the south of the Propylaea. The Parthenon in the background.

Section of the Cyclopean (Mycenaean) rampart and retaining wall of the beginning of the 5th century B.C. at the bottom of the ditch south-west of the Parthenon.

a. Mycenaean access: incisions on the rock.

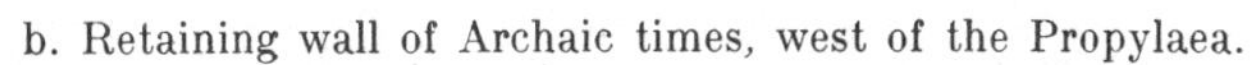

b. Retaining wall of Archaic times, west of the Propylaea.

a. The northern retaining wall of the access, time of Pericles.
b. Southern boundary of the access, time of Pericles (vertical cut in the rock).

a. Pittakes' Staircase.

b. Pittakes' Staircase (lower portion).

Altar of Apollo Agyieus(?) east of the Beulé Gate.

Base of the monument of Agrippa.

West face of the Propylaea.

East face of the Propylaea.

Outer south-west corner of the pre-Periclean Propylon and steps from the platform.

a. Sector of the pre-Periclean Propylon and of the Cyclopean (Mycenaean) rampart.

b. Internal face of the south-west corner of the pre-Periclean Propylon.

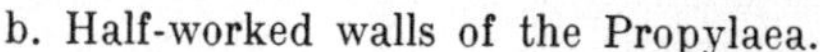

a. Base of an Ionic column from the Propylaea.
b. Half-worked walls of the Propylaea.

Cofferings of the ceiling of the Propylaea.

PLATE 18

North-east corner of the Propylaea.

«Bosses» on the north wall of the Propylaea.

View of the Propylaea from the north-east. Windows in the Pinakotheke dating from the Frankish period.

Sunset from within the Propylaea.

Surveying the Saronic gulf from the vicinity of the Nike Temple.

The Nike Temple from the north-east.

The Nike Temple, south-east corner.

South-east corner of the Nike Temple. Gods depicted on the frieze.

Sanctuary in the form of a double alcove on the west side of the Nike Bastion.Sector of the Cyclopean (Mycenaean) rampart.

Small Temple of Athena Nike, Archaic times.

a-b. Sanctuary of Brauronian Artemis.
Grooves and poros-stone blocks from the eastern section.

a. Sanctuary of Brauronian Artemis, overall view westwards
b. Entrance to the Sanctuary of Brauronian Artemis.

a. Northern limit of the Sanctuary of Brauronian Artemis. Rock cut vertically.

b. Stone structure upon the rock profile of the Sanctuary of Brauronian Artemis.

North-east corner of the Chalkotheke (only grooves) at the point of contact with the steps west of the Parthenon.

Chalkotheke from on high.

Poros-stone blocks from the foundation of the Chalkotheke.

PLATE 34

The Parthenon from the north-west.

Southern pteron of the Parthenon.

The interior of the Parthenon after rain.

The Parthenon from the north, before its restoration.

South-west corner of the Parthenon.

Plaque of the west frieze of the Parthenon (upon the building).

Metope of the Parthenon, the westernmost on the south side (*in situ*).

. Metope of the Parthenon, the westernmost from the north side, the so-called «Annunciation» (*in situ*).

Diagrammatic reconstruction of the acroterium of the Parthenon.

a-b. Fragments of acroteria from the Parthenon.
c. Lion head from the north-west corner of the cornice of the Parthenon.

West pediment of the Parthenon. Kekrops and his daughter (*now copies*)

The right edge of the east pediment of the Parthenon. Horses of the Moon (copies).

a. Capital from the Parthenon.

b. Capitals from the Parthenon belonging to a subsequent repair.

Position of the base of the chryselephantine statue of Athena in the Parthenon and hole for securing the central mast.

PLATE 48

Curves of the crepidoma of the Parthenon.

The main «Parthenon» and the western portal of the building.

Ecclessiastical murals on the wall of the Parthenon (old photograph).

Diagrammatic reconstruction of the preceding paintings.

Retaining wall near the south-west corner of the Parthenon.

a. Capital from the oldest Parthenon or the Old Temple, near the southern rampart.

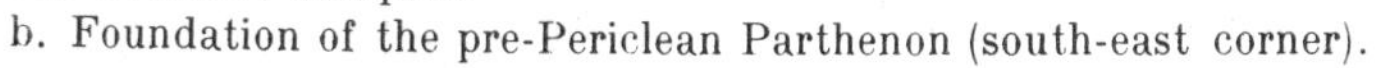

b. Foundation of the pre-Periclean Parthenon (south-east corner).

Ruins of the Temple of Rome and Augustus from on high.

a. The dedicative inscription from the Temple of Rome and Augustus.

b. Hypotrachelium of column from the Temple of Rome and Augustus.

a. Site of the Sanctuary of Zeus Polieus (grooves in the rock).

b. Ruins of the Sanctuary of Pandion preserved in the Museum basement.

The Erechtheion from the south.

PLATE 58

North porch of the Erechtheion.

North porch of the Erechtheion.

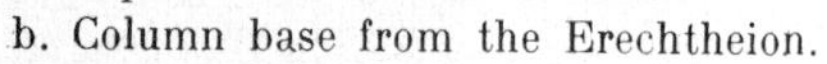

a. Capital from the Erechtheion.
b. Column base from the Erechtheion.

a. Ceiling of the north porch of the Erechtheion.
b. Decoration of the ceiling of the Porch of the Karyatides.

Portal of the north porch of the Erechtheion.

Porch of the Karyatides from the east.

. Porch of the Karyatides from the east.

Karyatides, the south-west corner.

PLATE 66

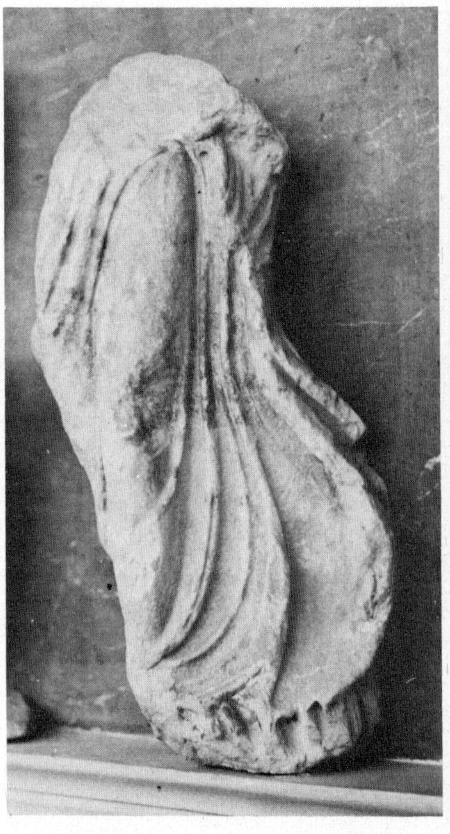

. a-b. Figures from the relief frieze of the Erechtheion (Acropolis Museum).

a-b. Figures from the relief frieze of the Erechtheion (Acropolis Museum).

The Erechtheion from the south-west.

Restoration work on the Erechtheion.

a. Ruins of the Old Temple from on high.

b. Column base from the little temple of Geometric times.

a-b. Capitals from the Old Temple.

a. Arrephorion.
b. Secret staircase from the Arrephorion.

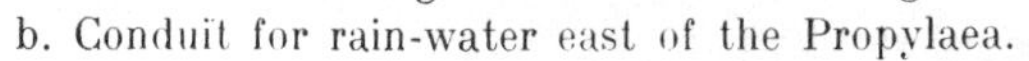

a. Ruins of buildings in the north-west region of the Acropolis.
b. Conduit for rain-water east of the Propylaea.

Foundation of the Kimonian rampart.

The Themistoclean rampart of the Acropolis from the north.

The Beulé Gate of the Acropolis from outside.

The Frankish tower in an engraving of Turkish times.

a. Turkish inscription chiselled on an architectural member from the Erechtheion.

b. Cuts in the rock for the reception of stelae, bases etc.

Cut for the votive Gaia Karpophoros (Fructiferous Earth) and inscription.

Decoration of the base of Athena Promachos: «egg-and-dart».

Epistyle from the small temple of Pandemos Aphrodite.

The Acropolis and the Parthenon seen from the Philopappos hill.

The Parthenon and the Odeion of Herodus Atticus.

The access to the Acropolis (1977). The Propylaea. The Bastion and the Temple of Athena Nike (Victory).

PLATE IV

The Temple of Athena Nike (Victory).

Looking at the Parthenon through the Propylaea.

PLATE VI

The N. wall of the Pinakotheke (Picture gallery) of the Propylaea.

Propylaea. NE. corner of the entablature of the main building.

Interior of the Parthenon. View to the East.

PLATE X

The Parthenon seen from the NW

The W. part of the Parthenon,

Parthenon. West. frieze.

Erechtheion. A view from the East.

Erechtheion. Porch of the Korai (Karyatides).

Erechtheion. Porch of the Korai (Karyatides).

Erechtheion. Porch of the Korai (Karyatides). A view from the NE.

ARCHAEOLOGICAL GUIDES OF THE GEN. DIRECTION OF ANTIQUITIES AND RESTORATION

1. Carl Blegen - Marion Rawson, The Palace of Nestor (translated into Greek by G. A. Papathanasopoulos). Athens, 1967 (2nd edition).
2. Agnes Sakellariou - G. A. Papathanasopoulos, National Archaeological Museum. A. Prehistoric Collections. A Brief Guide. Athens, 1964 (in Greek).
3. N. Platon, A Guide to the Archaeological Museum of Heraclion. Athens, 1964.
4. N. Platon, Führer durch das Archaeologische Museum von Heraklion. Athen, 1964.
5. Agnes Sakellariou - G. A. Papathanasopoulos, National Archaeological Museum. A. Prehistoric Collections. A Brief Guide (translated into English by Helen Wace, Elizabeth Wace - French and Ariadne Koumari - Sanford). Athens, 1964.
6. A Concise Guide to the Acropolis Museum. Athens, 1965 (1st edition) (in Greek) (out of press).
7. A Concise Guide to the Acropolis Museum (translated into English by Helen Wace and Elizabeth Wace - French). Athens, 1965 (2nd edition).
8. The American School of Classical Studies, A Guide to the Athenian Agora (translated into Greek by S. Platonos). Athens, 1965.
9. Agnès Sakellariou - G. A. Papathanassopoulos, Musée Archéologique National. A. Collections Préhistoriques. Guide Sommaire. Athènes, 1965.
10. Guide Sommaire du Musée de l'Acropole. Athènes, 1966 (épuisé).
11. Agnes Sakellariou - G. A. Papathanasopoulos, Archaeologisches Nationalmuseum. I. Vorgeschichtliche Sammlungen. Kurzführer (übersetzt von Maria Herrmann). Athen, 1966.
12. Kurzer Führer durch das Akropolis - Museum (übersetzt von Char. Neumann). Athen, 1967.
13. S. Karouzou, National Archaeological Museum. Collection of Sculpture. A Catalogue. Athens, 1967 (in Greek).
14. S. Karouzou, Musée Archéologique National. Collection des

Sculptures. Catalogue descriptif (traduit par X. Lefcoparides). Athènes, 1968.

15. S. Karouzou, National Archaeological Museum. Collection of Sculpture. A Catalogue (translated into English by Helen Wace). Athens, 1968.
16. Guida Breve del Museo dell' Acropoli (trad. di Dina Peppas - Delmusu). Atene, 1967.
17. St. Alexiou - N. Platon, A Guide to the Archaeological Museum of Heraclion. Athens, 1968 (in Greek).
18. A Catalogue of Casts and Reproductions. Athens, 1975.
19. St. Alexiou - N. Platon, A Guide to the Archaeological Museum of Heraclion. Athens, 1968.
20. P. Auberson - K. Schefold, An Archaeological Guide to Eretria (translated by P. Themelis). Athens, 1973.
21. St. Alexiou - N. Platon, Guide du Musée Archéologique d'Héraclion. Athènes, 1969.
22. St. Alexiou - N. Platon, Führer durch das Archaeologische Museum von Heraklion (übersetzt von G. Kokula). Athen 1969.
23. S. Karusu, Archaeologisches Nationalmuseum. Antike Skulpturen (übersetzt von Char. Neumann). Athen, 1969.
24. I. Vokotopoulou, A Guide to the Museum of Ioanninon. Athens, 1973 (in Greek).
25. A Concise Guide to the Acropolis - Museum. Athens, 1967 (in Greek) (2nd edition).
26. Guide Sommaire du Musée de l'Acropole. Athènes, 1968 (2nd edition).
27. Agnes Sakellariou - G. A. Papathanasopoulos, National Archaeological Museum. A. Prehistoric Collections. A Brief Guide (translated by Helen Wace - Elisabeth Wace - French and Ariadne Koumari - Sanford). Athens, 1970 (3rd edition) (reprinted in 1973).
28. A Concise Guide to the Acropolis Museum. Athens, 1970 (in Greek) (3rd edition).
29. Carl Blegen - Marion Rawson, The Palacc of Nestor (translated into Greek by G. A. Papathanasopoulos). Athens, 1970 (3rd edition).
30. G. Dontas, A Guide to the Archaeological Museum of Corfou. Athens, 1970 (in Greek).
31. Sp. Marinatos, A Brief Guide to the Temporary Exhibition of the Antiquities of Thera. Athens, 1971 (reprinted in 1972).

32. Sp. Marinatos, A Brief Guide to the Temporary Exhibition of the Antiquities of Thera (translated by Elly Arditis). Athens, 1971 (reprinted in 1972).
33. G. Dontas, A Guide to the Archaeological Museum of Corfou (translated by Helen Tsigada). Athens, 1972.
34. G. Dontas, Guide du Musée Archéologique du Corfou (traduit par Christiane Zoulas). Athènes, 1973.
35. C. Davaras, Sounion. Athens, 1973 (in Greek).
36. M. S. Brouscaris, The Mouments of the Acropolis. Athens, 1975 (in Greek).
37. Ancient Cypriote Art. Athens, 1975 (in Greek). Ancient Cypriote Art. Athens, 1975 (in English).
38. Byzantine Murals and Icons. Athens, 1976.
39. M. Brouscaris, The Monuments of the Acropolis (translated by A. Doumas). Athens, 1977.
40. M. Brouscaris, Les Monuments de l'Acropole (translated by P. Starakis - Roskam). Athènes, 1977.